Women in the Life of Crazy Horse

By **Gary W. Wietgrefe**

Produced by GWW Books
Rapid City, South Dakota

Cover Artist

In 1983 Homer Ignatius "Wambli Haca" Chief Eagle (1935-1989) sketched a beautiful, unnamed, mysterious maiden on an old, thickly-painted prison wall. Since the defunct jail is not accessible to the public, on November 2, 2025, a sheriff's escort allowed me to take a photo of Homer's maiden which appears on the cover of this book.

Underprivileged Homer, at age seven, lost his mother in childbirth. Grandparents, Alfred and Eva Night Pipe Chief Eagle, reared Homer and his nine siblings.[1]

The unfinished drawing was sketched while Homer was awaiting trial at the Tripp County Courthouse, Winner, South Dakota.[2]

Some have called Homer's unknown beauty, "The Lakota Mona Lisa."

Rather than let Homer's art flake into omission, I want readers to imagine Crazy Horse's mother and women in his life while immortalizing a talented, yet unknown, Lakota artist, Homer Ignatius Chief Eagle….Gary W. Wietgrefe

For permission requests contact the publisher.
GWW Books, 1811 Sunny Springs Dr., Rapid City, SD 57702.
Website: www.RelatingtoAncients.com
Email: gwwbooks@outlook.com
Quantity orders: special discounts are available on quantity purchases by schools, book clubs, organizations, businesses, and others. Submit a request at www.RelatingtoAncients.com, or gwwbooks@outlook.com.
Print credits: Book production: GWW Books, Rapid City, SD.
Cover drawing by Homer Ignatius, "*Wambli Haca*", Chief Eagle.
Cover design by Gary W. Wietgrefe
Font: Garamond
Name: Wietgrefe, Gary W, 1953---, author.
Title: Women in the Life of Crazy Horse

Identifiers: Paperback ISBN: 979-8-9941968-2-3

Subjects: Nonfiction: History
Classification: 1. ET150 Cultural Heritage/Native American
2. HIS036090 History/United States/State & Local/Midwest/SD;
3. BIO022000 Biography & Autobiography/woman;

First Edition. First Printing. Printed in United States of America.

Dedicated to forgotten women.

Contents

Character Profile[1]		
Relationship	Name(s)	Birth/Death
Self	Curly, Ca-oha, Light Hair, His Horse Looking, Crazy Horse	1840- Sep. 5, 1877
Father	Among the Trees, Crazy Horse, Waglula (Worm)	1810--1882
Mother	Rattling Blanket Woman	1814-1844
Stepmother	Iron Between Horns	1826--1884
Stepmother	Kills Enemy	1827—1877
Stepmother	Red Leggins	1829—1905
Sister	Looks at Her	1837—1901
Sister	Laughing One	1837--??
Sister	Tangle Hair	1837-1901
Sister (or first cousin)	Esther Smoking Woman	1859--1930s
Half-brother	Young Eagle	1843--??
Half-brother[3]	High Horse (Iron Between Horns' son)	1843 or 1849--1869
2 half-sisters		>1844--Died
Half-brother	Little Hawk	>1844--1870
Mistress (wife of No Water)[2] May 1870	Black Buffalo Woman	1844--
First wife M. 1871	Black Shawl	1845-1927
Second Wife M. July/Aug. 1877	"Nellie," "Ista Gli Win = Brown Eyes Woman," Helen, Helena, Ellen Larrabee, Larribee, Laravie, Laribee, Larvie, (in French L'Arrivee),	1853-1928
Daughter (of Black Shawl)	They Are Afraid of Her (also great aunt's name)	1871-1873
Child of Black Buffalo Woman[3]	A girl (her 3rd or 4th)	1870/71--

[1] Sources have inconsistent dates, names, and relationships.
[2] Relationship ended in 1870.
[3] Black Buffalo Woman had a girl months after running away with Crazy Horse.

Introduction

Crazy Horse is not the main character but an essential sub-character in this book. Through him you will get to know the **Women in the Life of Crazy Horse**.

The oft quoted proverb, "Behind every great man there's a great woman," certainly applies to Crazy Horse.

There are books, many historic, many fanciful, of Indian and Army battles, aligned and enemy chiefs, wins, scattered locations, details, and dates of their main character Crazy Horse.

Book-after-book of the famous Lakota warrior, women, if even mentioned, never rise above trivial characters behind cousins, subchiefs, and those he battled.

Not here.

Through these interesting women get to know the daily life, trials, and temptations on the open prairie of **Women in the Life of Crazy Horse**.

Clarifications

My lineage is European. Though I lived in South Dakota my whole life, I do not and will not claim that what I write will represent all terms or dialect, cultural, social, or spiritual meanings as if I was born into an Indian culture. I was not. Please forgive me where I should have stated a sentence or situation differently. In the nineteenth century and before, women were mainly known through their husbands as is true here. Quotes from authors and sources clarify context and are used for critical review of a topic or situation.

- Buffalo is used in lieu of American bison (*Bison bison* L.).
- Indian, not in any way to degrade a race of people, is used to aid reading flow rather than using Native American, Indigenous people, Redman, Native Redmen, pre-European People, pre-Columbian People, Aboriginal Americans, Amerindian, First Nations, Assorted Tribespeople, and the like.
- Spellings of various words, especially names, have been used to aid reader flow and minimize distractions of substitute spellings.
- Tipi is a term used rather than teepee, tepee, lodge, dwelling, tent, abode, Native

structure, Plains shelter, wigwam, mobile home, camp domicile, yurt, and etcetera.

- White is used to describe people that are not Indian.
- Woman or women are used. Those terms are never intended to degrade. Readers get distracted with interchangeable terms like female, lady, dame, squaw, gal, gentlewoman, madam, womankind, adult female, or other words that would be perplexing and diminutive in various contexts.

I have found no quotes from Indian women who knew Crazy Horse. Quotations from other authors were inserted to clarify a situation on the supportive role of **Women in the Life of Crazy Horse**.

Chapter 1

Getting to Know Crazy Horse

Why can a man be so famous and we hear so little about the women in his life?

There are reasons.

Before we get to the relationships, what led Crazy Horse to make marital decisions?

According to a biography, **Crazy Horse—The Lakota Warrior's Life & Legacy**, Crazy Horse was a member of a relatively small band of Miniconjou (pronounced in English as *Minni-CON-jou*), a division of the Lakota speaking a dialect within the Siouan language.[4] Other sources mention his father was Oglala and his mother Miniconjou.[5,6]

Any place in the world though the ages and today, it's easier to find a mate that speaks the same language. Coming from a small family band complicates selection of a spouse. To keep a viable family, genetic diversity is necessary. Mating someone other than your sibling or cousin was necessary.

Again, relying on genetic diversity, it was common to have parents from two different tribes.

By 1840 (some report his birth as late as 1845) when Crazy Horse was born, Siouan speakers were a large group of individual nations including Osage, Omaha-Ponca, Nakoda, Lakota, Dakota, Crow, Mandan, and etcetera. They were in what is now Kansas, Nebraska, South Dakota, North Dakota, Wyoming and Montana.

It is well documented Crazy Horse, in his late teens and twenties (marriable age), roamed a large area of Nebraska, Wyoming, Montana, and of course western South Dakota—especially the Black Hills where he was born around what is now Hot Springs.

As a warrior from a family of warriors, like his father and grandfather (both named Crazy Horse), Crazy Horse (the youngest) could speak with many of the tribes he fought against. Courting or capturing a potential wife from the Ponca or Crow was not unheard of at the time.

A wife or daughter captured by Indians was one of the biggest fears pioneers had heading west on the Oregon Trail from the 1840s to the end of the Civil War (1965). A young Lakota warrior, like Crazy Horse, in his early twenties would have been someone feared by them.

Many books on Crazy Horse focus on the last years of his life—when he was in his thirties before and after his rout with U.S. Army General Armstrong Custer.

A well-known secret is that the youngest Crazy Horse was actually called Curly until given his father's name when proven as a warrior.[4]

Curly?

Lakota have long straight black hair. Right?

Yes.

Hmmm?

Who was in the tipi nine months before Curly was born?

Relationships Crazy Horse had may become more obvious with this background.

Lakota tradition did not add a suffix, like Senior (Sr.), Junior (Jr.), or III. Usually after an event or accomplishment, names were simply bestowed on a son in Lakota culture recognizing a different person. It's not like

---

[4] No records exist of Crazy Horse birth. Historians date it between 1838 and 1845. Based on earliest confirmed dates, I have used 1840 as his birth year referencing 100-horse winter count, his mother's age at his birth, his father's statement of 1840 birth, oral history, and He Dog's (1840/42-1936) claim he and Crazy Horse were born in the same season on same year quoted during He Dog interview July 7, 1930.

they had mailboxes where the post office had to put mail in the correct generation's box.

Back to Curly--pre-Crazy Horse.

Rattling Blanket Woman married Crazy Horse (the father) between 1836-1839.

Was she white?

No, but…according to the Edward Clown Family's Crazy Horse biography, his mother

> "Rattling Blanked Woman had a smooth, light complexion and long sandy-brown hair. (His father) had a dark complexion and black hair," (Matson, p. 32).

Until the 1840s her tribe, Miniconjou (meaning Plants by the Water), was located in central South Dakota along the Missouri River. For at least a century, French fur traders had been trapping, trading, traversing, and living with local tribes.

Archaeology has shown that European manufactured beads, originally known as *pony beads,* started showing up in native settlements around 1700. Lakota women still cherish and use colorful beads in clothing and especially moccasins.[7]

In 1743, a century before Crazy Horse, Pierre Gaultier de La Verendrye or his sons placed a metal plaque on the bluffs above what is now Fort Pierre, South Dakota claiming the territory for France.[8]

Crazy Horse's mother's tribe remained in French-claimed territory until Napoleon Bonaparte sold what was known as the Louisiana Purchase to the United States October 1, 1800.

It was common for fur traders to marry Indian women where they traded.

> "French traders came from Canada or Saint Louis, Missouri, and one man might have a wife in each of several tribes with whom he traded," (Sneve, p. 23.)

Lewis and Clark's Corps of Discovery documented interactions with local tribes, including Lakota, in their 1804-1806 journey.

Consequently, it is quite likely Crazy Horse's mother had French, English, or at least European blood.

Was that unusual?

No.

Sioux in western Minnesota Territory (now eastern South Dakota) had been trading pelts for supplies for a hundred years before Crazy Horse was born.

Just like the Cheyenne River was named after the predominant tribe west of the Missouri river, the Big Sioux River in eastern South Dakota was similarly named.

Not only did the Sioux trade with the French and British, they intermarried with whites and fought against the United States decades before Crazy Horse was born.

One prominent Sioux Chief, Waneta (a.k.a. The Charger) in the early 1800s ruled the area where I was born—Brown County in northcentral, South Dakota.[9]

Waneta was a Yankton Sioux of the Cut Head Band who fought for the British from the Dakota plains as far east as Fort Meigs, Perrysburg, Ohio in the War of 1812.

Eye color: Waneta's older sister was Ista Totowin (Blue Eyed Woman) which means their father, Red Feather, had likely married a British, or European woman.

After the War of 1812, Chief Waneta went to England to be presented to King George III (1738-1820) as loyal British supporter.

After the United States won the war, Waneta aligned with the U.S.

It is certainly likely that Crazy Horse heard campfire stories about Waneta's South Dakota chiefdom as one the seven affiliated Sioux tribes.

Waneta, like Crazy Horse, was later invited to Washington, D.C. after fighting the U.S. Army. Waneta went twice.

Why?

During the Arikara War of 1823, Waneta fought for the United States. Arikara lost.

After signing the Minnesota Treaty of 1825 and Treaty of Prairie du Chien the same year, Waneta met the U.S. sixth president, John Quincy Adams, before he sat for a painting by well-known Indian artist, Charles King Bird.

A decade later Waneta met President Martin Van Buren (who was in office 1837-1841).

As will be mentioned later, Crazy Horse, like Waneta, was invited to Washington, D.C. several times. It wasn't because he had light skin and hair, it was his ability to align with the needs of his followers over his personal distrust of whites.

Not only was Crazy Horse called "Curly" into his teens, but he was also known as "The Light-Haired Boy" (the title of chapter one of Kingsley Bray's book).[5]

Okay, we know that Crazy Horse had curly, light hair when he was young. Although, it was not unusual for Lakotans to have mixed blood, perhaps being named Curly motived the teenager to claim his place in the Lakota warrior tradition.

He obviously did.

---

[5] Curly also called Light Hair at birth since that was also the color of his mother's hair. He was named Crazy Horse at age 17.

There are other factors that would have motivated young Crazy Horse.

About a decade before Crazy Horse was born, the fur trading and military post, Fort Pierre Chouteau, was established (1832) and became the largest fur trading post in the United States.[10]

Though Fort Pierre was established in 1817. In 1831 the Yellowstone was the first steamboat to traverse that far north on the Missouri River. Commercial freight moved into Arikara Territory recently claimed by the Sioux.

In 1844 Rattle Blanket Woman (Crazy Horse's mother) died.

Lakota had replaced the Cheyenne and other Plains tribes as the western-bound gold hunters traversed what became Lakota territory. The California gold rush started in 1848.

Treaty of Fort Laramie which established Indian territorial lines was signed September 17, 1851. It established land claims by the Sioux, Crow, and other tribes.[11]

Millions of buffalo, Lakota's main food, roamed the Dakota Plains. They did not need food brought up the Missouri River though they needed grains and vegetables grown along the Missouri.

Times were changing. Dramatically. New-comers, territory lines, transportation, technology, warfare (bow and arrow to rifles), all impacted Crazy Horse's young life.

Proving himself apparently took priority over finding a wife and settling down…though another man's wife interested Crazy Horse.

The Dakota Territory was established March 2, 1861, when Crazy Horse was a young man of twenty-one. That was a man's voting age. Women and Indians could not vote.

In 1862 the Union Pacific became the first Railroad to transvers Nebraska. At age twenty-two Crazy Horse had already fought skirmishes in Nebraska.

After the Civil War (1861-1865) as the American bison were being decimated, cowboys began driving cattle into the Plains.

By the time he was in his mid-twenties, Crazy Horse was exposed to many people, white and various Indian tribes.

December 21, 1866, Crazy Horse and other Lakota horsemen acted as decoys in Red Clouds "Fetterman Fight" also known as *Battle of Hundred Slain*, and *Fetterman Massacre.*

Crazy Horse got used to winning. At the time Fetterman Fight was the worst U.S. Army loss in the Plains. It took place in territory claimed by the Crow in what is now southern Sheridan County in northeast Wyoming.

Out hunting for food with diminishing buffalo, protecting his tribe, and battling invaders, left little time for Crazy Horse to hang around tipis and court young beauties.

In May of 1870 Crazy Horse did find time to head out of camp on a hunting trip with his cousin, some buddies, and Black Buffalo Woman (Red Cloud's niece and No Water's wife). (Bray, 130).

Chapter 2

Written Language

Crazy Horse was such an important character in Lakota history. Why aren't there better records of him and his family?

Those interested in writing about Crazy Horse can come up with very good questions, but answers are usually not given, not easily accessible, parsed, slyly avoided, and sometimes well researched with dead ends.

Why?

In order to understand the women in Crazy Horse's life, a few details need to be explained.

Have historians in the past century and a half tried to ignore him?

No.

In fact, considering the books, after books, after books written about Crazy Horse, I may suggest his life is the most well documented of any Lakotan.

Why then are so many details of his family, his whereabouts, and his marital relationships not well documented?

There are five primary reasons:

1. The Lakota language was an oral language, not written.
2. Until treaties were signed there was no written tribal or U.S. Government census or other records of Lakotan family connections.
3. Many of his family and tribe were killed.
4. Crazy Horse and his family were very leery of giving personal information to whites.
5. Women were sub-characters in Lakota culture.

Lakotans have a written language now. When was it written and by whom?

Christian missionaries followed fur traders. Evangelizing, missionaries followed Sioux west as they moved from their traditional territory around the western Great Lakes (Wisconsin and Minnesota) into the Dakotas during the 1700s.

A sketch artist, Frank Blackwell Mayer, from Baltimore, Maryland, traveled to Minnesota to witness the signing of the Sioux treaties of 1851. Attempting to provide background to those treaties, Colin Mustful in

2016 summarized Mayer's work about the first Sioux written language.

> "(Connecticut missionaries) Samuel and Gideon Pond settled (in present day Minneapolis, Minnesota)…(and) recognized the need to put the Dakota language into written form. …(The) first to assign letters to the Dakota language…Samuel Pond completed a small grammar and dictionary of three thousand words. Dr. Thomas Williamson (a Yale graduate in medicine) …arrived in May of 1834….and wife, Margaret, were sent to Lac qui Parle (western Minnesota) to prosecute the teaching and civilizing of the eastern-most Dakota bands."[12]

"Eastern-most" emphasizes that Dakota Sioux occupied what is now eastern South Dakota.

According to Mustful, Mayer knew of missionary Riggs as the 1851 Treaty translator but apparently he was not aware of the works by Presbyterian missionary, Stephen Return Riggs (1812-1883).

Riggs not only thoroughly learned the Sioux language, but translated over fifty volumes of literature, textbooks, catechisms, Scripture and hymns from English to Dakota when he lived along the Missouri River.

Perhaps Riggs' most linguistic accomplishment was a 16,000-word Dakota Language Dictionary.[13]

Without a written language there was no daily calendar nor clear genological charting of Sioux relationships—not even dates of birth.

To complicate matters, great aunts and uncles that lived nearby were called grandparents, aunts were sometimes called mothers, and cousins often reared by the same mother were called siblings.

Before recorded (written) history was the Old Stone Age.

> "We do not attempt to reckon its duration by centuries or millenniums.... The man of this epoch was in a way an artist. Hundreds of specimens of drawings, chiefly of animals on bone or on ivory have been discovered," (Myers, pp. 4-5).[14]

History had not yet been written, but rocks tools became more polished and refined.

> "The North American Indians were in this stage of culture at the time of the discovery of the New World," (Meyers, p. 5).

First Sioux writings were drawings (usually on hides) known as "winter counts." They were kept, year after year, and used to highlight special things that happened during a year and were recorded for the large winter tribal gatherings where fur traders attended to exchange goods for pelts and hides.

The common way of passing tribal history, myths, and family relationships were by oral tradition.

Various tribes throughout the North American continent have their own oral stories. I believe women had the most responsibility to pass on culture and tradition. Why?

First, though it varied by tribe, women were responsible for the settlement and were around night and day.

Women tended to live longer than fighting and hunting men which allowed them to teach stories over a longer lifespan.

Lastly, women were responsible for rearing children—boys and girls. Some stories circulated among women. Tribeswomen taught both genders social, cultural, traditions, and ethnic stories regardless of gender.

If a tribesman, father or grandfather, died during a hunt, women would provide family genealogical and geographical continuity.

> "…(about 1640) the Dahkotahs were further (west) than those tribes that dwelt along Lake Michigan. Later, in 1670 the Nadouessi (Dahkotahs)…dwelt on the shores and near the great river Mississippi…. (By 1837) the territory of the Sioux of the plains (Titonwans) extended from the Mississippi to the Black Hills…." (Holley, pp. 27-28, 32).[15]

Some tribes, like the Sioux, split over time into many different bands and moved to different geographies. The longer a tribe lived in one area, the more consistent the myths allowing family stories to maintain consistency.

Oral stories changed to fit new geography.

For example, the Sioux, as they moved west from the Great Lakes, changed their origination myth.

On the other hand, the Nootka Tribe of Vancouver Island, Canada had a secret Society of Women that was made notable in the book **Daughters of Copper Women** by Anne Cameron originally released in 1981.

Nootka society was facing a generational end. Stories were going to die with the last member of the Society of Women.

Cameron wrote the book to finally make public oral Copper Women stories of Klim Otto—a consistent Pacific Ocean current from California to the Aleutian Island chain. Klim Otto is a feminine name.

> "...She never changes speed and she never changes directions; and she's always there, now until forever. The life span of a woman is eighty years; and there have been 187 ½ lifespans since *Klin Otto* was revealed to Copper Woman. ...(The) Old Woman was grown at the time. She is now 15,000 years old and that's how long we've been on this coast," (Cameron, p. 112).[16]

That tribe's tradition and related stories were from a pre-European era in a different geography than the western Dakota Plains of Crazy Horse's era.

> "French explorer, Pierre Radisson, met Santee in 1660 when they resided near the lakes and woods of the Mississippi River. They were the mother tribe who called themselves Dakota," (Sneve, p. 3).[17]

Even Sioux origin of man stories logically changed with geography.

One Sioux spiritual story on the origination of man involves red rock. The Sioux, including Lakota, lived in what is now Minnesota in the seventeenth century. The town of Pipestone, in western Minnesota, has red rock exposed by glaciers that removed topsoil. The historic pipestone rock is still mined today to make Sioux pipestone smoking pipes.

Pipe-smoking was a traditional Sioux ceremony in decision-making councils during critical peace-making events before treaties were signed.

Man, according to this story, was created when a snake crawling on the red rock ate a bird egg about to hatch and suddenly a thunderbolt struck the red rock. The Great Spirit grabbed the piece of pipestone that flew up and formed the first man.[18]

As the Sioux moved west, myths and stories they told moved to new locations.

While in Nebraska, William "Buffalo Bill" Cody was told by an Indian it took three times for the Great Spirit to form the perfect man using a furnace.

First attempt, the clay was left in the oven too long and formed a black man. Realizing his error, the next attempt the Great Spirit removed the clay man he formed too early which became the whites. The third attempt the man came out just right and called the noble red man.[19]

Another story, the Great Spirit created the first people who lived in Wind Cave (Lakota call Maka Oniya = breathing earth).

Geographically Wind Cave, the largest cave system in the world, is located in the southern Black Hills of South Dakota. Wind Cave National Park was created in 1903.[6]

According to the myth, those original people had to stay in the cave because earth was not ready for them. Through trickery, one emerged…and eventually became a buffalo. Once the earth was ready, people were led to Wind Cave exit, saw buffalo tracks and were instructed to follow the buffalo for everything they need to survive.[20]

Briefly summarized here, these are the types of oral campfire stories Crazy Horse would have heard. He

---

[6] Wild buffalo now graze in the expansive 34,000 acre park.

was a spiritual man, but not a "medicine" man or spiritual leader like Sitting Bull.

One wonders which version of these myths Crazy Horse would have told his daughter.

I claim writing is artificial memory. Computers, cell phones, and cloud data storage are all forms of artificial memory.

> "Memory is a needed skill when survival is at stake," (Wietgrefe, Learning p. 294).[21]

Today could someone travel the states of South Dakota, Montana, Wyoming, and Nebraska without a map? Crazy Horse did—all from memory—no maps.

> "…Attention raised to its highest power remains fixed in the memory; that which is learned listlessly is lost easily…," (Eggleston, p. preface).[22]

Crazy Horse lived, dreamed, and contemplated in a spiritual realm as he desired to eventually reestablish his own reservation.

Times changed, especially after his death.

Without writing, radio, television, and computers, storytelling was evening entertainment around campfires. During the day, especially when teaching a lesson grandfathers and fathers would tell stories with a life's lesson to train boys. Sioux women would do the same for girls and young boys.

Reservation children were forced into schools and despite all the stresses caused to parents and children, a great compliment was paid to the Indians living in South Dakota in a 1915 school textbook.

> "The word '*Dakota*' means "A Republic of Friends.' No more honest or upright class of primitive people ever were found, and none, when educated, show more splendid intellect and character," (Johnson, p. 8).[23]

Children respected elders as they were taught.

I will use an example from a 2025 book by my friend, Victor Swallow. I worked with his daughter, Vikki, to publish Victor's stories for his eighty-sixth birthday in the book entitled, **Lakota Life After the Buffalo**.[24]

That book has forty-two oral Lakota stories dating back into the mid-1800s. Many of the stories were passed to him from his mother, as told by his mother's mother, and his mother's mother's mother (that would have been Victor's great grandmother).

Women had less chance than men of being killed by enemies or wounded by buffalo. It was up to mothers and grandmothers to pass on family stories.

Regarding the importance of passing on oral stories, Mr. Swallow wrote,

> "...Mother, Lizzie Two Bulls-Swallow, who was born in 1907...(and) was the second

> generation out of the wild. Her grandparents were born out on the prairie somewhere. Mother was interested in history. She told of many events that happened in her early life."

When transacting business with fur traders, Indians used sign language. From the mid-1800s as Lakota children were educated, sometimes forced into boarding schools, children learned English by reading, writing, and were required to speak only English in and around school.

They were punished when Lakota was spoken in schools. Victor Swallow wrote an oral story about his grandmother visiting his mother at boarding school.

> "Mother's mother came to see her children (at their Rapid City, SD, school). When she spoke to the matron, she had her daughter Dora translate."

Sioux, and especially Crazy Horse's band of Lakota Sioux, led a nomadic lifestyle. Doing so created clashes in areas claimed by other Indians.

In their original territory, Sioux enemies, Chippawa (a.k.a. Ojibwe) and Cree became the stronger tribes, perhaps by acquiring guns from the incoming French and British.

For survival and seeking peace, Sioux bands considered it best to move west into what is now western Minnesota and eastern North and South Dakota.

Eventually, the Teton band (a.k.a. Lakota) followed the buffalo and roamed as far west as the Rocky Mountains in what is now Wyoming and Montana.

Obviously, as the Sioux moved west, they created many enemies with tribes that had permanent settlements (i.e. Arikara sometimes called Ree) along the Missouri River. Others, like the Crow, considered the Lakota as trespassers onto their hunting grounds.

Chapter 3

Horses

Before horses, women were beasts of burden. They moved their household to winter and summer grounds on foot, papoose (cradleboard) on back and dog drag by their side.

In 1700s the Sioux acquired horses from the Arikara who likely got them from their distant southern relatives, the Pawnee, who likely traded for them or they captured wild Spanish horses.

Obviously, horses of different sizes and different breeds were acquired at different times, in different places, by different people, for different reasons.

With ammo and guns, mostly bows and arrows, the Lakota moved west across the Missouri River. Sioux's western movement had been restricted by those tribes that roamed the western Plains who also fed off the buffalo (i.e. Crow and Cheyenne).

Plain's travelers (early Plains fur traders) were discrete and highly competitive—not wanting others to know where they traded with Indians and where they trapped pelts.

Other than company records, fur trappers and traders (a.k.a. mountain men) were extremely independent and their travel records sparce.

Fur traders had been traveling western South Dakota perhaps as early as the late 1600s. Based on French exploration records and a dated metal plate unearth above Fort Pierre, SD, (by children playing on a Missouri River hill) in 1913, Verendrye brothers claimed the territory for France.[7]

It is important to this story to remember the Sioux language speakers traditionally in the Great Lakes area did NOT have horses. They did not travel far. Dogs were beasts of burden and also a source of meat.

Dogs could pull small loads by travois (a dog harnessed to two sticks tied together with leather). When a particular settlement moved, limited materials were taken and obviously they had only small tipis.

---

[7] Pierre Gaultier de Varennes, sieur de La Verendrye and four sons operated fur trading posts in Canada and what is now North Dakota as early as the 1730s. Records indicate they explored central and western South Dakota west through Wyoming to the Montana Rocky Mountains in 1742-43 and claimed the area for France.

Before the horse, buffalo and elk, traditional favorite meats, were carried from the spot they were downed by arrow to the family campsite—often miles away.

Since there was no alternative, Lakota were conditioned to carry heavy loads—a common trait before horses.

Archeological physiologists often use the figure for human carrying capacity at fifty pounds for thirty miles in a day.

> "Evidence from professional archeologist Nancy Malville shows that grain transported throughout the Paquime'/Anasazi/Meso-American system from the growing fields to storage facilities ranged at least 60-90 miles to the occasional much longer distance and weights carried ranged from 100-150 pounds. ...Tlingit packers over the Chilkoot Trail in the late 1800s (Klondike Gold Rush trail British Columbia, Canada to Alaska) ranged up to 200 pounds (per person)," (Fisher).[25]

Lakotans were fit, lean, and strong.

Before horses, out of necessity, four men would have each carried about 150 pound quartered elk from distant hunts through woods, across hills and prairie to their camps with waiting wives and hungry children.

Buffalo quarters would have weighed twice as much as elk. That meant Lakota groups traveled and set camps near grazing buffalo before hunts to minimize the load-carrying distance.

Once Sioux acquired horses, a travois load, known as a *pony drag*, was scaled larger than dog drags. In preparation to use horses, they cleaned longer tree poles to mount behind horses which allowed them to build larger tipis using horse travois poles.

> "The Indians at first called horses 'elk-dogs' and used them for food. But soon the Plains Indians saw the horses merit as riding animals. So Tribal wealth in time was judged by the size of the Indian's horse-herd. With the aid of travois poles, a horse could carry 200 pounds," (Longstreet, p. 5).[26]

One man needed four horses to transport a whole buffalo back to camp.

Travel gear on hunts was organized, loaded and unloaded by women. Berries were harvested in-season during travels. Women kept a keen eye for wild turnips, wild onions, herbs, and other useful plants.

Distance traveled per day was farther in the semi-arid western Plains. It was preferrable to camp by water at night. Women had to haul the water for camp use.

As a result, horses allowed more extended family members to live and sleep in a larger tipi—organized by women.

Roaming from stream to stream, thriving on balanced meals of plenteous buffalo, dried plumbs and berries (like chokecherries), and wild roots (like turnips), Lakotans became the tallest of known tribes of the 1800s.

Starch needed in diets was stolen corn or acquired by trade. Settled tribes along the Missouri River grew corn, gardens, and maintained constant protection from roving hunter-gatherers.

The Saga of Hugh Glass, August 1823:

> "Arch foes of the Rees, the Dakota were said to have returned for repeated harvesting of Arikara farm products, as various kinds of corn and other plantings of the fled tribe ripened. Undoubtedly, the Indians Glass encountered were on their way to make another agricultural raid," (Myers, p. 147).[27]

After getting horses, taller tipis were welcomed. Food supply equals population growth. As in any historical culture, people living on plenteous food and balanced nutrients grew taller and had more children. Rearing children was women's responsibility.

Specific for this book, Victor Swallow wrote an oral story passed on from his great grandmother about the Lakota transition after Crazy Horse's death.

> "...Three Lakota men that my mother knew lived through an ever changing era from roaming free and hunting to the Government killing all the buffalo to the Little Big Horn Battle in Montana in 1876. They experienced the Ghost Dance that came about that brought hope to the Lakota people of a returning nomadic lifestyle," (Swallow, p. 106).

The energetic, caring, ever-roaming, and fierce fighting Crazy Horse, destitute with about nine hundred followers could not survive after the buffalo were decimated.

Being nomadic, they grew no grain. Prairie fruit, berries, and wild roots were scarcer in the remote areas of western South Dakota, southeast Montana and northeast Wyoming where they could best avoid the U.S. Army.

In the absence of buffalo, especially after the Civil War (1861-1865) when Crazy Horse was in his early twenties, cattlemen gathered vast herds of Texas steers and cowboys, many boys in their teens, drove cattle north into the Plains.

Those cattle supplied beef to eastern markets collected at the new rail stations. However, many of the cattle were contracted by the U.S. Army to feed the Indians confined by treaty to agencies and later reservations.

Protein, mainly beef, and other goods were allotted to individuals under treaties.

Fortunately, Victor Swallow wrote down some of the oral stories told by his grandparents. Those stories were not only about people and dates, but life.

> "In the years after the breaking of the 1868 treaty that shrank of the Great Sioux Reservation then occurred Little Big Horn Battle, killing of Crazy Horse, and the buffalo were gone. The Lakota were confined to small reservations completely dependent on the U.S. government for staples to keep them alive. In 1890 beef rations for the Rosebud Brulés were cut to two million pounds and the Oglala by one million pounds," (Swallow, p. 110).

Just because the Lakota way of life changed so quickly, did not mean they didn't look for hope. Chiefs and elders continued to pass on stories and look for hope.

After Crazy Horse died, the Ghost Dance emerged. Mr. Swallow wrote:

> "They were a people whose former way of life was destroyed. They were destitute. Lost with no hope for tomorrow. Furious. Along came this movement from Utah, the Great Dance," (Swallow, p. 110).

To better understand Crazy Horse's era, a bit more historical background is needed.

This, nor other Crazy Horse stories, would exist if the Sioux had not acquired horses. Secondly, there were no Sioux or Lakota given the "Horse" name before they got horses.

Even during the Crazy Horse era, Lakota followed naming tradition of previous years when horses did not exist.

Besides the three generations named Crazy Horse, in the late 1800s, "horse" began appearing in more Lakota names.

There was a Red Horse who surrendered with Spotted Elk in 1877. Living Bear Hoarse, Blue Horse, Horse Bear, and Sitting Horse all surrendered with Crazy Horse in 1877. High Horse, the son of Iron Between Horn, was a half-brother to Crazy Horse.

Women apparently were not given a "horse" name. That must have been a masculine name. Besides, women walked next to the dog and pony drags.

After they acquired horses and moved west, the Sioux eventually aligned with the western tribes, like Arapaho and Northern Cheyenne. Sioux, especially Crazy Horse's Lakota band, were expert horsemen when fighting white settlers, miners, and the U.S. Army.

Sioux had no money. Horses were currency.

Wives were purchased and debts settled with horses including Crazy Horse's mother, Rattling Blanket Woman.

Now for allotments.

What are allotments, and how did they provide records of family ties?

Some of my research, especially on Crazy Horse wives, relies on ration and allotment records. As you will discover later, rations (food, clothing, bedding, etc.) and land allotments were tracked by the male surname.

U.S. Census records of anyone living in the U.S. referred to wife and children using the husbands/father's name. That was typical historically through Biblical and other cultural tracking systems.

Please keep in mind until U.S. Army census, Lakotans only had one name. No surname. Consequently, Crazy Horse was his first and last name. Generally, the father or mother would take another name if their son or daughter was privileged enough to bestow the parent's name.

Crazy Horse's father also had one name "Crazy Horse." He was first called "Among the Trees." At some point, the father gave his son the name Crazy Horse. Then, Among the Trees became Crazy Horse (II) he had the right to give up his name Crazy Horse to his son, he (the father) then became known as Waglula (Worm).

Therefore, there was only one person at any one time that had the name Crazy Horse. Hence, wives in this book are of Crazy Horse (III).

(A fellow, Greasing Hand, perhaps in order to maintain government rations, later claimed the name Albert Crazy Horse.)

Okay. Why were rations and allotments so important?

Without an Indian or his family member's name recorded in government records, that person did not receive food, clothing, bedding, medical care, eventually land parcels, and etcetera as provided in treaties.

Lakota were a roaming, meat eating people. Buffalo had been indiscriminately decimated. Lesser available wild meats (i.e. elk, deer, bear) numbers declined significantly. That forced Lakotans like Crazy Horse, Sitting Bull, Red Cloud, Spotted Tail and all Plains leaders onto reservations by military defeat, starvation, lack of shelter, lack of cloths, and lack of bedding.

Imagine Lakota women trying to keep their kids clothed, moccasins made, and shelters patched.

To end this segment, allotments may be best summed up by referring to a 2006 document by Lakota genealogist Kingsley M. Bray in his **Notes on the Crazy Horse Genealogy, Part 1**:

> "...Rudimentary census counts of Lakota bands did not begin until thirty years after Rattle Blanket Woman's tragic death,[8] this is not surprising. She died too early to be named on allotment records, introduced in the early 20th Century, which routinely identified the allotee's parent," (Bray).

Fortunately, because of allotment records, and oral stories from contemporaries of Crazy Horse's era, much has been researched and written about Crazy Horse. That is the only way I was able to find tidbits on women for this book.

To understand how this one unique individual, Crazy Horse, developed spousal relationships, we must first learn about his parents.

---

[8] Rattling Blanked Woman, Crazy Horse's mother, died in 1844.

Chapter 4

Rattling Blanket Woman

Rattling Blanket Woman, the mother of Crazy Horse, has been described as "…famously beautiful and a magnificent runner…" (Bray, 10).

Could the cover sketch of this book be Rattling Blanket Women? We'll never know. Homer Chief Eagle never told anyone, nor did he inscribe her name on his incomplete sketch. I like to think Homer got out of jail before he was able to finalize his masterpiece.

Running was a special skill developed by the Lakota. Perhaps they became the westernmost Sioux tribe because they honed the skill of running well before they had horses to chase buffalo.

Americans had no racing beast of burden before the Spanish arrived with the horse. (Maybe they had dog races.) Instead, they hunted by foot, delivered goods by foot, and raced by foot for fun.

The most well-known American ancient runners that survived into the twenty-first century are the Rara' Muri—the Running People better known by the Spanish reference Tarahumara who live in the Copper Canyon of northern Mexico.

> "According to the Mexican historian, Francisco Almada, a Tarahumara champion once ran 435 miles.... Other Tarahumara runners reportedly went three hundred miles at a pop. In 1971, an American physiologist trekked into the Copper Canyon and was so blown away by the Tarahumara athleticism that he had to reach back 2800 years...not since the ancient Spartans has a people achieved such a high status of physical conditioning," (McDougall, p. 15)."[28]

My wife and I were able to travel the Copper Canyon in 2025 and see how the Tarahumara lived in cave-dwellings and ran in traditional dress—not much more than a breechcloth. They were surprisingly tall people with physiques of habitual runners browned in the sun.

It takes a mind, body and willingness to run.

Lakota have that ability as demonstrated by Pine Ridge, South Dakota running legend, William Mervin "Billy" Mills (1938--). As a virtual unknown from the poorest area of the U.S., he qualified for the 10,000 meter run in the 1964 Olympics in Japan.[29]

Following at a record pace, Mills, an Oglala Lakota, surged past the two leaders on the last lap setting a new world record. He was the first American to win the 10,000 meters which was fifty seconds faster than he had ever run as an announcer asked, "Who is that guy?"

Billy Mills still makes Pine Ridge proud.

Little is known of Crazy Horse's mother, Rattling Blanket Woman, but one thing noteworthy she was a good runner. Her son picked up her determination.

Rattling Blanket Woman's father was Black Buffalo (1850-1815) and her mother may have been White Cow or Pretty Voice Woman. Rattling Blanket Woman had a brother (Lone Horn) and two sisters [Good Looking Woman/Lady, and Looks At It (a.k.a. They Are Afraid of Her)].

Crazy Horse's mother's family seems to confirm she was Miniconjou and possibly even a sister of chief Spotted Tail.

Of importance to this story is that Crazy Horse, after being shot by a jealous husband, recovered in community of his mother's family though his mother died twenty-six years earlier. This background gives confirmation he maintained strong ties with his mother's relatives—although he was considered an Oglala Lakota.

In 1840, Rattling Blanket Woman was proud to produce a son for her husband whose "heart was full" as he could now pass on his Crazy Horse legacy. In return,

Rattling Blanket Woman tried to conceive another child over the next four years—without success, (Matson, pp. 32-35).

It is well documented that Crazy Horse had light hair, some sources report light brown hair. Since Lakota have dark straight hair, Crazy Horse must have had somewhat wavey hair to be nicknamed "Curley" until his father transferred his name "Crazy Horse" and took the name Worm for himself.

Detail of Crazy Horse's hair was extremely likely to be inherited trait of his mother. Some suggest his light skin and hair were traits received from an illegitimate white-man father.

There are many cases in Crazy Horse literature where his extended family may exaggerate or underplay a characteristic or incident. Some do not even mention his fling of 1870. In attempt to make Crazy Horse a bit different his mother's "sandy" hair is mentioned but rarely this father's black hair.

For a Lakota, who were apparently the tallest of any North American Indians, Crazy Horse had a small build—maybe around five feet five or six inches.[9] His father was at least six foot.

---

[9] Poor sources report Crazy Horse was seven feet tall making him an imposing figure leading war parties. Not true. Likely, those authors were confusing Crazy Horse with his cousin, Touch The Clouds (6"9-7.0')—the youngest son of Lone

Size in battle has little do with fighting ability or bravery. Perhaps his smaller stature magnified his need to be a bold brave.

The Edward Clown family gave a detailed report how Crazy Horse II (a.k.a. Worm) stole horses loaded with buffalo meat from Crow hunters as a dowery to purchase his wife, Rattling Blanket Woman, from her father, Loan Horn (Matson, pp. 28, 32-35).

Sioux women who found, preserved, and prepared food, dismantled and erected tipis and maintained them were often traded as property. As you will read later, wives went with hunting parties to attend to domestic affairs (i.e. camp setup and preparing foods). Men hunted, protected, waged raids, and smoked pipe.

Time after time U.S. Army journals of traders reported that Sioux woman had constant tasks, worked all the time, and cared for children. Perhaps Virginia Driving Hawk-Sneve put it best in her book, **Sioux Women—Traditionally Sacred**:

> " French explorer, Pierre Radisson[10] reported that the Sioux women seemed to be

---

Horn. Also, Hump, his father's friend and mother's brother, was about six feet four inches tall. Hump was a long-term mentor of young Crazy Horse.

[10] Pierre-Esprit Radisson (1640-1710) at the age of eleven was captured by the Iroquois, learned their language, escaped, and developed the fur trade for France and England helping to establish the Hudson Bay Company. As a French,

> drudges who attended to all chores while the men hunted and fished…(compared to) European tradition in which women did little physical work and hunting and fishing were (men's) leisure-time pursuits."

It seems like too many authors, especially early exploration journalists, reported how Indian women could be relied on to do many tasks and were overworked.

Women picked berries, bore children, healed the wounded, kept settlements organized, joined hunts, prepared meat and hides, and stripped the dead after battle.

Given this background, it is reasonable to understand why ever-independent Crazy Horse sought a women's support in his waning days.

Sioux men loved women and protected them. They were not just property to be traded as indicated by the original relationship between Crazy Horse's parents.

White man's alcohol caused marriage difficulties then and still does. More on that later.

The family's detailed story of Worm's dangerous effort to get horses demonstrated his love for Rattling

---

English, and Iroquois speaker, Radisson delt with many Indians including the Sioux of the Great Lakes and upper Mississippi River.

Blanket Woman. He went far beyond a casual desire for a wife to risk life to get his first wife.

Rattling Blanket Woman was most likely illiterate and her children too young to tell their mother's story. Historians speculate why she killed herself.

I will leave those tales for others.

Some have reported that Rattling Blanket Woman's sister, Good Looking Woman, offered to be Worm's wife as a replacement to raise siblings, Laughing One (daughter), Crazy Horse, and High Horse (another son).

When Crazy Horse was about four years old, Rattling Blanket Woman hung herself with a rope or leather strap in 1844. That happened after his father, Worm, returned with his two teenage wives and their younger sister.

Though four-years-old when his mother died, Crazy Horse had a warm place in his heart for his mother and her people. Her death, and his father's wives may be why he delayed courting until in his late twenties.

Chapter 5

Worm

Let's take a look at Crazy Horse's father.

Rattling Blanket Woman was Crazy Horse's mother and her only husband, Worm, lived longer than their son.

Worm is the English version of Waglulu, the name taken when the name Crazy Horse was transferred to his son.

Lakotans are obviously interested in carrying on their cultural history. For tribal membership, they must know their family connections. If they have no known tribal documents to justify membership, tribal benefits, like health care, are prohibited, or at least thoroughly questioned.

Some, like Victor Swallow mentioned earlier, have written down some oral stories of his grandparents who were contemporaries of Crazy Horse.

Others, like Lakota elder, Black Elk was a second cousin to Crazy Horse and also was at in the Battle of Little Big Horn. (Their fathers were cousins.)

A well-known Christian convert and Oglala Lakota holy man, Black Elk, was interviewed at length in the early 1930s.

The most popular book of Black Elk's memories was translated to English by his son, Ben Black Elk. They were transcribed by Enid Neihardt (John Neihardt's daughter) and published by Nebraska poet, John Neihardt in 1932 under the title **Black Elk Speaks**.

Since John Neihardt was a poet, he took liberties with his daughter's transcripts. Though **Black Elk Speaks** are true stories of the man, Neihardt's book, as published, must be considered historical fiction.

The University of Nebraska's republished 2014 edition with 196 pages of annotations and appendixes made an excellent attempt clarifying what Black Elk actually said (as per transcripts) and what Neihardt took poetic liberty when botching Black Elk's words.

Caution must be used with this book and others. Authors, like me, rely on numerous research documents and constantly deal with historical errors, misunderstood situations, and sometimes deception.

I am trying to do my best, but I can only rely on records, however sparce, to bring understanding to the **Women in the Life of Crazy Horse**.

Many have questioned when Crazy Horse was born. His mother died before he could understand and relate to his birth year. That is where parent's memories are important.

Given the shock of his son's death, it is highly unlikely a father would have any reason to not tell precisely the birth of his cherished son.

On the date Crazy Horse got killed, Worm, Crazy Horse's father, said to U.S. Army Lieutenant H.R. Lemly that his son, Crazy Horse, was born in the fall of 1840.[30]

The last surviving Lakota colleague of Crazy Horse was He Dog. In a July 7, 1930, interview He Dog said:

> "I and Crazy Horse were both born in the same year and at the same season of the year. We grew up together in the same band, played together, courted the girls together, and fought together. I am now 92 years old, so you can figure out in what year he was born by your calendar."[31]

That should have meant they were both born in 1938 but somehow He Dog's statement was calculated to mean they were both born in 1840 (though 1938 is a possibility and contrary to nearly all other references).

Let's touch a bit on the background of the Crazy Horse family and to which Sioux were they most connected.

Crazy Horse seemed to have a strong, perhaps stronger, connection with the Miniconjou than the Oglala Sioux. Though his father, Worm, was Oglala Sioux and associated with them, it could be that Worm's mother, as stated before, was Miniconjou.

It would make sense that Worm would take wives from a different Sioux division. Interbreeding with close relatives was highly discouraged.

Crazy Horse's stepmothers were reported to be Sicangu (Burnt Thigh People) and not specifically in the general band Miniconjou Lakota. Others suggest his stepmothers (his father's second, third, and possibly forth wives) were Miniconjou.

Mid-1800s were troubled times for Sioux. The 1862 Dakota War (a.k.a. Minnesota Massacre) strained relationships within various Sioux bands. In doing so, various leaders and followers split between different geographies.

Furthermore, U.S. Army demands forcing Sioux onto reservations created conflicts between chiefs. Some chiefs felt more comfortable with other chiefs not in their band.

As evidenced, Oglala Lakota Crazy Horse's fight against reservation life was in conflict with Red Cloud, the main Oglala Lakota chief and spokesman.

Red Cloud tried to make life better for his followers at the Red Cloud Agency near Fort Robinson, Nebraska.

After the Great Sioux War (1876-1877), Red Cloud and his followers, Oglala Lakota, Northern Cheyenne, and Arapaho tried to peacefully conscribe to government allotment at his Agency—a precursor to reservations.

Crazy Horse's mother was Miniconjou, and if his father's mother (grandmother) had been Miniconjou, it would stand to reason that Crazy Horse would closely associate with his Miniconjou connections.

That strong Miniconjou connection was confirmed by Crazy Horse.

How?

He was taken to them to recuperate after being shot by No Water.

Though Worm was Oglala Lakota, he, like his famous son, felt comfortable with other bands. Specifically, Worm and his Sicangu wives are buried at Rosebud, South Dakota which is associated as a Sicangu community.

Too many forced and optional transfers occurred between the different bands before, during and after the Red Cloud War (1866-1868) and before the end of the Great Sioux War in 1877. With wives in the background, confirmation of which were in a specific Lakota band is speculative at best. Besides they often mixed.

Crazy Horse had multiple wives. He learned from his father who had at least three wives. After the death of Crazy Horse's mother, Rattling Blanket Woman, Crazy Horse was raised by his stepmothers.

Who were they?

First, they were sisters.

How did it happen that Worm married three sisters?

The oldest stepmother was Iron Between Horns. She was born in 1826.

Kills Enemy, born in 1827, was the one that died in the same month shortly after Crazy Horse—in September 1877.

Red Leggins, born in 1829, was only fifteen when their father, Corn, gave his two daughters to Worm. Red Leggins wanted to be with her older sisters and went with Worm to Worm's home where wife, Rattling Blanket Woman, was waiting his return.

When Rattling Blanket Woman's only husband, Worm, returned from a buffalo hunt with three young women, it further strained their marital relationship. Sometime later Rattling Blanket Woman committed suicide.

Having three more women in his tipi, what impact did that have on young four-year-old Crazy Horse?

That dramatic event needs a background story.

Please keep in mind four things: buffalo roamed vast areas. Indian hunters could not always be assured they would know where the buffalo were grazing.

Some days buffalo were found in large herds. Next week when hunters went out they could find none, or perhaps only a lone bull. They may have moved toward a better water supply or had been scared off during a competitor's tribal hunt.

Secondly, buffalo hunting tribes roamed. Therefore, Lakota were roamers. They settled temporarily by water where buffalo were grazing in proximity. Bulls, the heaviest animals with the most meat and most utility, would often isolate outside of breeding season.

Thirdly, because buffalo roamed, and other Lakota villages roamed, one village's hunters may not know where the other villages were hunting.

Fourthly, as Lakota Sioux moved west, they often came in contact with other roaming tribes, like Crow who were fierce enemies. Crow village warriors would decide to attack a Lakota village—maybe for food, maybe for wives, maybe just because they considered Lakota trespassers.

Anyway, in 1844 Worm was out hunting and either planned to visit another Lakota village under Chief Corn, or Corn's village was hunting buffalo in the same area preferred by Worm. It would have been common to recruit other hunters to pursue buffalo with slaughter and preservation done more efficiently.

When Worm happened to appear or was staying in Corn's village, Crow Indians attacked. Though the number of Crow warriors is not established, it is likely Worm expertly prevented the Crows from killing Corn, the chief and his daughters, although Corn lost his wife in the skirmish.

Worm may have been staying in the same Corn family tipi while visiting his encampment.

As an honorary reward, Corn gave his two virgin daughters, Iron Between Horns and Kills Enemy to Worm. The fifteen-year-old sister, Red Leggins, begged her father to allow her to be with her sisters. Worm returned to his village, undoubtably with buffalo meat and two wives and their sister.

Rattling Blanket Woman was shocked.

Sometime later, perhaps after Rattling Blanket Woman perished, Worm reportedly also married Red Leggins. Although it is likely Red Leggins later married another man and had children by him.

So, it is a bit fuzzy whether Red Leggins was ever a stepmother to Crazy Horse. At fifteen when he was four, Red Leggins obviously cared for him.

It was likely Rattling Blanket Woman and the three sisters, Worm's new wives, were all sleeping in the same tipi with Crazy Horse and his sisters.

Distance between Corn's village and Worm's village has not been established. However, Crow Indians apparently did not attack Worm's home village while he was gone—suggesting a fair distance from Corn's camp.

I speculate that it would have taken the thirty-three-year-old Worm much longer to return to his village with two teenage wives, seventeen and eighteen than it would have taken if he had returned by himself.

Lakota have a keen sense of humor—including silence.

Silence is a unique trait. Rattling Blanket Women and Worm's camp likely practiced silence around the tipi foursome, but camp gossip would have ran ramped out of earshot.

How much did Crazy Horse hear?

This would not be the last time camp gossip and rumors were heard in Crazy Horse's camp.

Two other events about women occurred in his life decades later that were deliberately withheld from Crazy Horse.

When others talk, talk, and talk, rambling as reported during treaty negotiations, chiefs listened to the interpreter intently, displayed a poker face (restrained expression), and were hesitant to respond. Younger chiefs yielded the floor to older chiefs when a response was required.

It was proper for younger women to hold their tongue when and elder women were speaking.

Eyebrows were most certainly raised in Worm's home camp when he left by himself to go on a buffalo hunt and returned with three teenagers. (Suggestions have been made that Worm only married the oldest before returning to his home camp.)

Silence would have been prudent around Worm and Rattling Blanket Woman. However, it's easy to imagine ribbing from friends even years later. For before returning from the buffalo hunt, he explored where no other man had gone.

During the days of Worm's return, it is not unreasonable to speculate on some intimate tipi activities consummating marriage.

Likely, Corn also gave Worm buffalo meat and other supplies for his daughters and their travel. Perhaps the foursome's move and festive activities were enjoyed during the trip.

I will leave Worm's chapter reporting his original wife, Rattling Blanket Woman, hung herself (Bray, pp 10-12).

Meanwhile, the three teenagers supported Worm's camp life while raising his daughters, Looks at Her, Laughing One, Tangle Hair, and son (Crazy Horse) and their other children, Young Eagle, High Horse, Little Hawk, and a couple other (unnamed) half-sisters that apparently died when young.

Speculation runs rampant by those trying to empathize with a husband that lost his wife due to suicide.

It was tragic.

One line goes that Worm spent four years grief-stricken. Other historians do not mention empathetic details.

Crazy Horse had some white blood. Some suggest that Worm had accused Rattling Blanket Woman of an affair with a white man while he was hunting buffalo and collecting other wives.

Another possibility: an author mentioned she was having an affair with her brother-in-law while Worm was having an affair with Rattling Blanket Woman's sister. (Bray, p. 10.)

Speculation?

Since Lakota tradition apparently allowed a man to have more than one wife, and a wife had the option of choosing another husband, history cannot be clear why Rattling Blanket Woman decided to take her life at the end of a rope.

No matter the reason, it happened.

No doubt, his mother's sudden death left a lasting impression on the four-year-old Crazy Horse.

Knowing background of his father and mother may shed light on the fiercely independent fighter who tried to maintain Lakota's traditional way of life that Crazy Horse visualized since youth.

Is that way he married much later than other Lakota men?

Is that why he took a mistress from her husband?

Is that why he married wives with completely different backgrounds, abilities, and tribal relationships?

Chapter 6

Bigamy and Polygamy

This book's title, **Women in the Life of Crazy Horse**, evokes the obvious question, did Crazy Horse and his father commit bigamy, polygamy or both?[11]

Yes. Yes. And yes.

Before being disgusted, it would be good to understand the Lakota tradition. Multiple wives was normal. Crazy Horse and his father were wildly independent. In their culture many caveats were allowed.

First, Worm, Crazy Horse's father, had at least two wives at the same time for thirty-three years.

Did losing his mother affect his other relationships?

---

[11] Bigamy: marrying one person while being legally married to another. Polygamy: At the same time, having more than one spouse.

Probably.

Like father, like son?

Not really.

There were major differences between father and son's spousal arrangements. My hunch is that Rattling Blanket Woman would have approved at least two of the three relationships of her son.

Times were changing.

Besides the dangers of killing buffalo, Lakota kept losing men to conflicts with Crow, Shoshone, Blackfeet, Pawnee, and later with the U.S. Army, miners, settlers, and cross-country travelers.

No record of the Lakota population demographics is available when the Sioux as a group fought Chippewa and moved west. Total population of Lakota women west of the Missouri River in the late 1800s outnumbered men.

Lakota's roaming settlements were quite small. Though marriage to a close relative was highly discouraged, marrying siblings of another family was common.

Crazy Horse's father, Worm, is only one example of marrying from another family line to minimize dangers of inbreeding.

Rattling Blanket Woman's death, her sister, Good Looking Woman, apparently offered to marry her husband, Worm, and raise Crazy Horse, even though Worm already had at least two wives. This speculation has been mentioned in other reports.

Not all Lakota men and women had multiple spouses. Records are not clear, but my hunch is that chiefs, and well-respected warriors, like Crazy Horse, would likely have had more wives than other lesser known or lesser respected Lakota men.

For example, one of the most famous Lakota chiefs who resisted the white invasion was Sitting Bull (1831-December 15, 1890). He was a spiritual leader (holy man), prophet, warrior, chief, and well-respected leader as Hunkpapa Lakota.

Sitting Bull (age forty-five), during the battle at Greasy Grass (a.k.a. Custer's Last Stand), at the time was much more influential than Crazy Horse (age thirty-six).

Why have more than one wife?

Importance and duties as a Lakota leader required Sitting Bull to move often, move quickly, and maintain camp decorum.

To cook and care for Sitting Bull's growing family's camp, needs like picking berries, drying meat, tanning hides, camp setup, childcare, stripping poles for horse drags, and serving husbands many guests kept his wives busy.

Sitting Bull had at least three wives but likely had five or more including Seen-by-her-Nation, Four Robe Woman, Light Hair, Snow on Her, Four Blanket Woman, and Her Holy Door. He fathered many children.

One of those children, Crow Foot, was killed along with Sitting Bull by Native American Tribal Police December 15, 1890.

Lakota Tribal Police were recruited within each tribe to keep order, break disturbances, and make arrests. Initially they reported to a U.S. Army officer and later to the Bureau of Indian Affairs.

Tribal Police are mentioned in the book of oral Lakota stories by Victor Swallow, **Lakota Life After the Buffalo**. Victor's maternal grandfather, Fred Two Bulls, performed in the Buffalo Bill Cody's Wild West Europe show that started in 1887.

Buffalo Bill's first ship carrying show material to England included ninety-seven Indians, eighteen buffalo, five Texas steers, four donkeys, a couple deer and ten elk.

Fred Two Bulls was popular in his family but not as famous as other Lakota performers in Wild Bill Cody's shows such as Sitting Bull, Chief American Eagle, and even Red Cloud.

Victor Swallow ended his oral Lakota tribal policeman story about his grandfather, Fred Two Bulls, with the propitious statement,

> "I often wonder how my peoples' life would be if the Government left us alone," (Swallow, p. 9).

Mr. Swallow indicated to me that his grandfather was not liked by some Lakota because he later became a tribal policeman.

Likely, the same situation existed at the time of Sitting Bull's arrest.

Bull Head and Red Tomahawk were the two police that each fired shots that killed Sitting Bull.

It was the prelude to the Wounded Knee massacre that followed December 29, 1890.

Crazy Horse had great respect for Sitting Bull but was killed before him.

The same cannot be said for Red Cloud. He had a different management style and was often irritated with the militaristic Crazy Horse.

Red Cloud, an Oglala Lakota chief, warred against white settlers, miners, and especially the U.S. Army between 1866-1868. The Army referred to it as the Red Cloud War.

Red Cloud was a pragmatist.

He traveled to Washington D.C., met world leaders, realized the outnumbered industrial white world of the east was well established, organized, was moving west supplemented by railroads, and maintained a massive army despite having just ended an internal Civil War.

All major cities in the east where Red Cloud traveled had larger populations that the whole Lakota nation.

He realized Whites would continue westward invasion into Lakota lands. Red Cloud did not like it but was committed to dealing with whites while helping his people.

Red Cloud had his own agency with four thousand Oglala Lakota, Northern Cheyenne, and Arapaho under his management.

Meanwhile, Crazy Horse wandered by attracting renegades to continue his devoted fight to maintain Lakota lands. They had different styles. Respect for each other was limited.

Even when Crazy Horse finally surrendered at the Red Cloud Agency (nearby Fort Robinson, Nebraska) May 6, 1877, with his 899 starving followers, Red Cloud was irritated.

Crazy Horse was the star.

> "In the months following the Crazy Horse surrender at Red Cloud Agency in early May 1877, the enigmatic chief remained the center of attention," throughout the Fort and Agency, (Hedren, p. 144).[32]

Crazy Horse and his followers accounted for about a fifth of the total Indians at Red Cloud Agency. With all the attention, Red Cloud had to deal with gossiping, minor chiefs' jealousy, and ensuring monthly rations.

Arrival of Crazy Horse and potential revolt created more stress for Red Cloud.

I brought up Red Cloud because he had only one wife and was married about fifty years.

The same cannot be said about Spotted Tail (1823-August 5, 1881). The Brule Lakota chief of the Spotted Tail Agency, also located in northwest Nebraska, was about forty miles from Red Cloud Agency.

Spotted Tail's first wife, Hears Horse,[12] some report her as Sees The Enemy (1825-1885) married him in 1842. In 1851 Spotted Tail married Julia Black Lodge (1840-1913).

Red Cloud didn't like Crazy Horse.

Likewise, subchiefs didn't like Spotted Tail. They were often jealous of his fame and interaction with the white men.

Unlike Crazy Horse, Spotted Tail was shot and killed by Crow Dog,

---

[12] Hears Horse is a rare exception where 'horse' is in a woman's name.

> "Purportedly to take vengeance against Spotted Tail for having stolen his wife…August 5, 1881," (Hedren, p. 165).

Accumulating wives created problems and life complexities for famous Lakota chiefs like Worm, Sitting Bull, and Spotted Tail, but apparently not for Red Cloud who had one wife.

Crazy Horse's women problems started late for a Lakota man. With all the events trying to maintain the Lakota roaming way of life, it would have been tougher without a wife managing his camp details and packing for travel.

Crazy Horse survived skirmishes against other tribes and the U.S. Army in Nebraska, South Dakota, and Montana—including the Battle of Little Big Horn without taking a bullet.

Interestingly, Crazy Horse's late start at seeking a wife nearly killed him with a bullet.

Chapter 7

Before Romance

The mistress saga of Black Buffalo Woman is not a secret. Crazy Horse's relationship with her is surprisingly well documented--not in all versions.

In fact, not surprisingly, some extended family did not address the relationship. Many versions refer to Black Buffalo Woman as the first wife of Crazy Horse.

You decide.

In the last chapter I mentioned Red Cloud was not keen on Crazy Horse. I gave several legitimate reasons why they didn't get along.

Another tidbit: Black Buffalo Woman was Red Cloud's niece—a daughter of his brother.

Red Cloud had established himself in the Red Cloud War which concluded in 1869. Red Cloud and a group of other chiefs went to Washington, D.C. in 1870.

For years, Crazy Horse did not want to develop relationships with whites or the U.S. Army. Whereas Red Cloud, as a leading Lakota chief, had regular meetings with them.

Other Lakotan took sides or were trying to decide if they should follow Red Cloud, Spotted Tail, Crazy Horse, Sitting Bull, or other chiefs.

One person that thought it was best to get along with whites was subchief No Water. It was well known that,

> "No Water was associated with the pro-American factions. He had been one of the akicita[13] recognized under the Harney agreement of 1856," (Bray, p. 130).

No Water was the husband of Black Buffalo Woman. They had three children and were still living together as a married couple in 1869-1870.

In 1865 at the Lakota Shirt Wearer Society ceremony, Crazy Horse had been awarded the title of Shirt Wearer for his Lakota values, warrior abilities, and he was a good representative of his tribe.

Apparently, No Water was also a Shirt Wearer candidate and was overlooked in favor of Crazy Horse.

---

[13] Akicita was a Lakota warrior and or soldier.

Jealousy over a woman may be too mild to describe the Crazy Horse/No Water relationship.

Chronologically, the year was 1869. Crazy Horse was twenty-nine and Black Buffalo Woman was twenty-five.

They liked each other.

Like starting a fire, a flicker becomes a flame and embers get hot before the fire cools.

Unfortunately, fire in Crazy Horse's first romantic adventure came from the end of gun.

There has been some fanciful stories of the Black Buffalo Woman/Crazy Horse romance.

- Some are romantic historical fiction.
- Others are oral family stories passed on to justify the escapade as a short-lived "marriage."
- Interestingly, some deliberately avoid discussing this major detail of Crazy Horse's love-life.
- Others appear to be truthful details.

I will follow the last point but relate other imaginative stories and flame-rich possibilities.

Those interested in history of a famous person may appreciate a few stage-setting cultural and practical conditions that existed on the Dakota Plains in the mid-to-late 19th century affecting Crazy Horse, his family, their tribe, and other Indian nations.

I will not bore you with Crazy Horse military activities, treaty dates, and other happenings during his adult life and romantic eight years (1869-Septeber 5, 1877).

What occupied Crazy Horse instead of marriage?

Crazy Horse traveled far and wide as a warrior and hunter. He must have tried to figure out a beneficial outcome for his eventual wife and family.

A lot happened in the Northern Plains around that period, including:

- Fetterman Massacre occurred on Crow Indian land (traditional Lakota enemies) near Fort Kearny, Wyoming on December 21, 1866. Twenty-six-year-old Crazy Horse and others functioned as decoys.
- Lakota fought the U.S. Army often with Arapaho Indians allies. Crazy Horse, Sitting Bull and others won the Battle of Little Big Horn, and killed U.S. Army General George Armstorng Custer, June 25, 1876.
- Ramifications of the U.S./Native American Treaties, including the April 29, 1868, signing of the Treaty of Fort Laramie, a.k.a. Great Sioux Reservation Treaty, affected why Crazy Horse fought, where he roamed, and eventually where he wanted to create his own reservation.

- Cross-country travelers/Lakota skirmishes over the Oregon, California, and Bozeman Trails all involved Crazy Horse directly or indirectly. For example a cow owned by a Morman, Christian Larsen, strayed into a tribal camp and was killed August 17 or 18th, 1854 by a visiting Miniconjou Sioux, High Forehead, resulting in the August 19th Grattan Massacre which started the First Sioux War.
- Pony Express operated through Indian lands from April 3, 1860, until October 1861. Buffalo Bill Cody was the most famous rider who later employed Red Cloud, Sitting Bull, and others in his European touring Wild West Show.
- Transcontinental telegraph was completed through Sioux claimed territory October 24, 1861. Crazy Horse was twenty. The singing wire was a technological shock to Lakota.
- U.S. Civil War (April 12, 1861-May 26, 1865): many war veteran troops were sent west thereafter to protect incoming settlers, caravans, reservation boundaries, railroad crews, and keep the peace between Indian and white factions.
- Sioux and others moved from Nebraska and Kansas to Oklahoma and South Dakota between 1873-1875.
- U.S., in fact the world, experienced and economic collapse in 1873 and lasted into the 1890s. All was related to money that the Lakota did not use.

Economic depression affected how Lakota land was taken, when the railroads paused construction, and somewhat delayed the prized buffalo's decimation.

- Transcontinental railroads were completed through the central and northern Plains. Central Pacific Railroad was completed May 10, 1869, which ran from Council Bluffs, Iowa to San Francisco, California. The second from the Great Lakes to the Pacific Northwest was celebrated with Northern Pacific Railroad's golden spike hammered into the ground September 8, 1883. Railroads continued through Sioux lands with completion of the Great Northern Railroad between Minneapolis and Seattle January 6, 1893.
- Recreational buffalo hunting occurred at the end-stops as transcontinental railroads progressed across the Plains into the mid-1880s. No wild buffalo were left to shoot when the third transcontinental Railroad was being built. By then beef cattle were the main protein.
- Decimated buffalo herds occurred from the 1860s to 1884. Documentation: millions of buffalo were slaughtered, some for hides, as I.G. Baker and Company transported 75,000 buffalo hides in 1876, 20,000 hides in 1880, 5,000 in 1883, and none at all in 1884 (Hedren, p. 99).
- Indians on rations hung around "Soldiers' Town." *Hang-Around-the-Fort* people was a derogatorily

term used by those, like Crazy Horse, fighting reservation life.

Crazy Horse would have been a conservative traditionalist, or non-Progressive.

Moving on, this is woman-based story.

It reminds me of a quote credited to visionary, Edward Creighton, who built telegraph lines including the first transcontinental telegraph line through Sioux country in Nebraska.

> "Our United States did not become a great nation because of the big things done by the Franklins, the Washingtons or the Jeffersons, whose names history remembers, but because of the small things done by the common people whose names history has forgotten," (Miller, p. x).[33]

Who were the forgotten women? Some saved Crazy Horse's life. More on three of them later. Black Shawl not only saved his life, healed his bullet wound, but became his first wife. Many don't know the first wife of hero, Crazy Horse. You will as this book unfolds.

As long as I brought up Edward Creighton and women, many don't know that his wife, Mary Lucretia Creighton, founded Creighton College (now University) in Omaha, Nebraska one year after Crazy Horse was killed. (Crazy Horse was killed September 5, 1877, and Creighton University was founded September 2, 1878.)

Creighton, a private medical, legal and business university, is one of the nation's most highly rated. Started and funded by a women, U.S. News and World Report ranks Creighton top "National 2026 Best Colleges."

There are many books including those referenced in this book's bibliography and index which provide helpful historical details of long-forgotten Sioux women.

Of all the books I've read about Crazy Horse, I don't remember seeing one quote from his mother, stepmothers, wives, or any Sioux women associated with Crazy Horse. May they be forgotten no more.

There are several reason why Sioux women are hardly mentioned in background stories. Women maintained camps. Men fought.

Historians tend to write about battles and men who won and lost. Women were peripheral, if mentioned at all.

For example, Edward Creighton's segment of the first transcontinental telegraph reached Julesburg, Colorado on July 3, 1861. (Crazy Horse was twenty-one years old.) That day Creighton's crew barely escaped a raging prairie fire by desperately driving their teams of oxen and supplies across the Platte River.

About a mile before Julesburg, Creighton noticed a few Indians standing by a newly planted telegraph post. He sent Matt, errand boy, to find out what they were up to. Of course, the first question Matt asked was,

> "'Are they Hostile?' Creighton replied: 'There's a few squaws among them. Indians don't take their women on the warpath,'" (Miller, p. 47).

As the story goes, the young Matt approached showing his hands that he had no weapon. A young Indian boy, about his age, stepped forward and said in sign language,

> "My name is Growling Cub. My Father is Black Hawk, a chief of the Sioux. These are my people. We come to look at white man's magic," (Miller, p. 48).

Creighton's crewman Matt explained how words were transmitted though the wire which was whistling in the prairie wind (the same wind blowing smoke away from them).

The Indians smirked, others laughed, someone suggested it was an animal—like a long snake, but most thought Matt was blowing smoke.

> "Why is the wire crying?' Growling Cub asked. 'The wire is not crying,' Matt told him. 'It is singing because it is happy as many messages of good cheer run through it," (Miller, p. 49).

This is an example of how women accompanied Sioux as they traveled across the Plains. But, in the whole story, boys to old men did the talking, not women.

The group listened to the wire humming in the wind and stood pondering the impossible.

> "At last an old white-haired Indian raised a knotty finger toward the line and said, 'The singing wire,'" (Miller, p. 49).

As is typical of Lakota, the aging man's short, succinct, simplified definition became the name of the book, **The Singing Wire**.

Basically, during what should have been the young married life of Crazy Horse, he was fighting a losing battle against U.S. interior expansion. Railroads, telegraph, gold rushes, and buffalo's demise was happening every direction Crazy Horse traveled the last twenty years of his life.

Many did not want to hang around the fort. They understood Crazy Horse's vision, but just like the singing wire, complexities of development was nearly impossible to understand.

Each year, with diminishing returns, Crazy Horse was ever seeking the disappearing buffalo that had sustained the Lakota since they arrived on the western Dakota Plains in the 1700s.

As you will read later, Crazy Horse's sister-in-law was involved with the reestablishment of the buffalo. It did not happen as Crazy Horse imagined, but it became reality in what should have been his lifetime.

Chapter 8

Clandestine Relationship

In the summer of 1869 the upcoming affair between Black Buffalo Woman and Crazy Horse was well known within Lakota circles. An ever-single, well-respected warrior getting encouraging cheers from a beautiful married woman was not ignored.

When did the relationship start?

Before Black Buffalo Woman married No Water?

Likely.

Wannabe Crazy Horse biographer and well-known novelist, Mari Sandoz (1896-1966) wrote the fanciful story **Crazy Horse: The Strange Man of the Oglala**.[34] In it she claimed Crazy Horse and Black Buffalo Woman were childhood sweethearts…since she was born.

Sandoz claimed:

> "Curley had been a small boy when Black Buffalo Woman was born. He remembered it because the one he called mother had stayed back with a woman on the day when people were moving…(with) a new little daughter for the brother of Red Cloud," (Sandoz, p. 113).

Now you know why many consider Mari Sandoz more a novelist than a biographer. Sandoz was born nineteen years after Crazy Horse was killed but writes as if she were present in 1844 when Black Buffalo Woman was born. She even reported what Crazy Horse thought as a four-year-old.

Sandoz wrote historic fiction at its best.

The quote above by Sandoz is why this book was difficult to write. What was fiction? What was fact? What was supposition? To be sure, I will not claim I have all facts straight, but I don't want to mislead readers either.

When a hero is a villain in a novel, the villain is justified or induced by love to cover misdeeds. Whereas the victim and his or her feelings are brushed aside as irrelevant.

Crazy Horse is the hero. No Water the victim.

The latter will lose his wife to an imprudent fling, whereas the backstory of lifelong endearment becomes acceptable…at least in Sandoz' version.

Sandoz historical novel goes on to build Crazy Horse's childhood connection to Black Buffalo Woman.

> "Young Curly looked upon the small thing as somehow belonging to his own lodge. …He tickled the corners of her little mouth (with a long spear of grass) until she woke and laughed.… (Later in adolescent years)…He threw plumbs at the girl… (Sandoz, pp. 113-114."

Nowhere have I found similar content in historical writings or oral stories passed down by Lakota relatives.

Unfortunately, plausible scenarios get repeated as if fact. Soon, with reference after reference, those scenarios are accepted as fact.

For example, it seems somewhat consistent and quite logical that No Water was away from home when Black Buffalo Woman left with Crazy Horse.

In fact, it is documented by several sources that it wasn't just Crazy Horse and his mistress. Instead, it was a small group of men, likely teenage boys, and at least two woman—Black Buffalo Woman and Black Bear's wife.

Except for scouting and warrior raids, it apparently was quite common for Lakota expeditions to include women. Who was going to dig turnips, pick berries, set up tipis, and cook? Women. Those were women's tasks.

After a successful hunt, women prepared the meal.

Consequently, it was not necessarily out of the ordinary that Black Buffalo Woman left the care of her three small children[14] with other relatives or women in their home camp when she left with the Crazy Horse group.

As the story goes, Crazy Horse had a long-time desire to wed Black Buffalo woman.

Years before, likely about 1865, Black Buffalo Woman had been courted for months, if not years by both No Water and Crazy Horse. Both were warriors of reputation. Both had often gone on hunting trips, scouting, military maneuvers, and raids to secure horses, weapons, ammunition, and food.

They disliked each other. Likely it was competition for beautiful Black Buffalo Woman. It seems apparent that Crazy Horse and No Water rarely traveled in the same group, or in the same direction. However, both supported the Red Cloud war party in 1862.

Complaining about a toothache (Sajna, p. 157),[35] No Water returned to camp. Some suggest his return was timed when he knew Crazy Horse would not be there. The purpose of his timed return was to marry Black

---

[14] Some sources have stated she only had two children at the time.

Buffalo Woman and move her into his tipi before Crazy Horse found out.

Getting a wife was not that simple. First, No Water had to have approval to marry from Black Buffalo Woman's father. Secondly, No Water had to meet the marriage price.

After the Sioux gained horses (about 1700), the Teton-Lakota roamed the central plains. Since they had a custom of moving more than the Sioux tribes in eastern South Dakota, Minnesota and Wisconsin, the Lakota had more need for horses to transport their camp using pony drags (travois).

Lakota became expert horsemen which elevated the horse to the most valued possession. Consequently, to get a bride, her father must accept the number of horses offered before the groom could take the daughter for marriage.

Beauty and chastity usually required more horses.

Asian, African, and European cultures had a long-established history of dowries where the bride's family had to accumulate and present to the groom a valuable bundle of goods for the groom to accept the bride.

In Lakota culture, it was just the opposite—dowry in reverse. The groom had to "purchase" (appease) the girl's father.

No Water was about seven years older than Crazy Horse. He may have been born about 1833 and Crazy Horse in 1840. That meant that No Water had more time to accumulate property, especially horses, than did the younger Crazy Horse.

Secondly, Crazy Horse apparently was not a person to place goods or property before integrity. Although Crazy Horse likely could have stolen as many horses as his father to gain a bride, that was not his style.

At some point, No Water arrived in camp with enough horses to appease Black Buffalo Woman's father.

For several reasons, I suggest their marriage occurred between 1862 to 1865. First, history confirms Black Buffalo Woman had two and possibly three children when she ran off with Crazy Horse. Second, we know the children were too young to be on their own, since Black Buffalo Woman divided her children between family and/or friends when she left.

Having someone look after young Lakota children in the mother's absence was customary. Had the girls been older, say ten or so, they would have stayed in their home tipi and cared for themselves—of course with a grandmother, aunt, or friend as a guardian.

Whenever the marriage took place, the family culminated the marriage and No Water went to his tipi with Black Buffalo Woman.

When Crazy Horse eventually returned to camp he quickly found out that his nemesis had married his sweetheart, Black Buffalo Woman.

Let's fill in a little more backstory.

Depending on the source, there are several scenarios. Where was Crazy Horse when Black Buffalo Woman married No Water?

- On a raid;
- On the warpath;
- Scouting; or
- Hunting.

The only thing I'm certain is what Crazy Horse wasn't doing. He was not raiding a white, Crow, or Arapaho camp to kidnap a wife. At his age, very late twenties, that would have been a likely scenario.

Since inter-family marriage was prohibited, Lakota men were honored when they returned from an outing with a new wife of different genetics. Into the 1860s, kidnapped white women were apparently considered a special reward.

The downside of white women was that they were not used to the women duties of a Lakota camp. They were not used to working with other women in household. Lastly, even though they were overworked, they didn't appreciate their husbands having other wives.

Another conflict in sources: when did Black Buffalo Woman leave camp, and "elope" with Crazy Horse?

Besides the discredited, Sandoz, likely Crazy Horse first met Black Buffalo Woman in 1857. That seems like a believable date. He would have been seventeen and she would have been fourteen.

Even if their camps jointly paused at a buffalo kill, teenagers at those ages would have paid special attention to the opposite sex.

Although the Crazy Horse/Black Buffalo Woman escapade is not firmly dated, those suggesting 1867, 1868, and even 1869 seem to be too early, though logical. The Treaty of Fort Laramie (a.k.a. Sioux Treaty of 1868) was signed from April through November 1868. It seems likely the pause allowed Red Cloud and warriors, like Crazy Horse, to return to their home camps.

Likely the flames of romance had built in the winter of 1869 into 1870. Perhaps the best source is He Dog a close friend of Crazy Horse. As He Dog was quoted before as saying, "…we courted the girls together…" (Hineman, p. 10).

He Dog was also interviewed by John Colhoff which confirms the spring of 1870 day of Crazy Horse's departure with Black Buffalo Woman.

He Dog and Crazy Horse returned from a battle with the ever-menacing Crow. The fight was referred to in

Lakota circles as '*When They Chased the Crows Back to Camp*' confirmed to be in the spring of 1870. He Dog said,

> "About ten days after that battle Crazy Horse started off with a smaller war expedition and No Water's wife went along with him," (Hinman, p. 14).

He Dog was reported to have a very good memory into his nineties. Within family and tribal circles, when someone would ask a historic question, they would send them to ask He Dog.

The He Dog quote above not only identifies the departure time of Crazy Horse and his mistress, but also why they left.

"…A smaller war expedition…" made sense.

First, they had just finished a successful rout of the Crow. Secondly, Crazy Horse and his group likely intended to head north on the east side of the Black Hills toward Slim Buttes where bison were still grazing in significant numbers.

Slim Buttes, in what is now Harding County, South Dakota, is a narrow rocky strip of pine forest. Basically, it is an isolated section of the Black Hills. On March 5, 1904, with 58,160 acres, it was designated Slim Buttes National Forest. Within a couple years it was absorbed into the National Forest Service and now part of Custer National Forest.

(Photo taken by Gary Wietgrefe September 14, 2025, south of Buffalo, Harding County, South Dakota.)

Two hundred years ago, Slim Buttes was considered Crow Indian territory. By 1870, Lakota, a permanent enemy of the Crow established northwest South Dakota as part of the greater Lakota-Sioux range.

On a personal note, when I was in my mid-twenties, I hunted that prairie and pine-covered area for deer and antelope. Antelope permits were easy to come by. Ranchers considered pronghorn antelope a pest as they can eat a lot of scarce grass fenced for cattle.

Cattle fences are no barrier for antelope. They are the fastest land animal in North America and can slip under barbed wire fences at a full run.

Although we lived two hundred and twenty miles east of Slim Buttes, that is an area my father, brothers, and I liked to hunt and camp.

I can relate to Crazy Horse and why his group headed for Slim Buttes. It provided shade for camping, ruggedness for hiding and diverse game.

Whitetail deer lived in the wooded area of Slim Buttes. In 1976 I had a Harding County whitetail deer permit and shot my last deer in Slim Buttes with a Remington 22-250.[15] Immediately outside the wooded buttes in the prairies is where mule deer and antelope continue to live.

One other unusual characteristic of Slim Buttes—it was an ancient forest of huge trees. I remember hiding behind a rocky petrified log waiting for deer.

In 1870, Crazy Horse, his mistress, and followers were likely looking for buffalo and elk as food for their war expedition. With buffalo and elk becoming increasingly scarce, notable game in that area would have

---

[15] My father passed away in the fall of 1980, before hunting season. To give him a break from work, my brothers and I liked to get our father away from our farm. Hunting Slim Buttes in the fall of 1979 was the last time I hunted deer and camped with my father.

been deer and antelope with fast-flying sharp tail grouse and prairie chickens as meat supplements.

Before No Water arrived at their camp, I want to mention a few of those that were on the expedition.

Black Bear must have had a fairly large tipi. It was the primary gathering place of the leaders. When No Water arrived, Crazy Horse, Standing Elk, and Touch The Cloud, Black Bear, Black Bear's wife, and Black Buffalo Woman were all in the one tipi.[16]

A few other men were resting from the day's ride. Likely their wives were preparing a meal. Young boys also were likely along. Their duties would have been fetching water, stabling and protecting the horses, and other odd jobs.

While others were visiting outside, and Black Bear's tipi group were engaged in conversation of the day's activities, No Water arrived.

The next minute changed Crazy Horses' life.

---

[16] Touch the Cloud and Standing Elk were cousins of Crazy Horse.

Chapter 9

Did they mate?

Here are a few reasons historians, extended family and commentators give for why Black Buffalo Woman left with Crazy Horse:

- No Water was a no winner.
- No Water left their home camp to buy more alcohol.
- No Water was known to drink and mistreat Black Buffalo Woman.
- No Water was on an expedition with Red Cloud.
- Black Buffalo Woman thought Crazy Horse could protect her from No Water.
- Crazy Horse, Black Bear and others would need women to support their hunting or military expedition.

Although some or all of those suggestions may have a hint of validity, it should also be noted that No Water was a close ally of Red Cloud. (I mentioned before

Red Cloud was frustrated with Crazy Horse.) The Clown family reported when the frustration really started.

> "Red Cloud felt that he had lost his influence over the young men because Crazy Horse had stopped listening to him during the war (1866-1868) over the Boseman Trail," (Matson, p. 69).

Lakota were a diverse roaming group under many chiefs. No doubt, Crazy Horse had independent thoughts of how to handle the "white" situation. Secondly, he had different thoughts than senior advisors about No Water's wife.

Before we get too far into the tipi shooting action, a timeline needs explored to understand if Crazy Horse had the opportunity to have an intimate relationship with Black Buffalo Woman. If so, how long were the two traveling together?

Roaming is key. Movement of a Lakota camp (hunting or miliary expedition with women along) would have been deliberate, slow, and purposeful.

The first priority would have been water. Horses need to drink a minimum of once per day. Drinking water twice or more per day would have been required on extended journeys.

The second factor was time to travel.

The third issue was securing food.

Those three issues are fixed.

A huge conflict arises from various accounts of where Crazy Horse was shot by No Water.

Some have suggested, "The Stronghold," (Matson, p. 68). Some readers may remember The Stronghold was the area in the Badlands of South Dakota near where the Wounded Knee Massacre occurred (December 29, 1890).

The Stronghold is located in the Badlands on the Pine Ridge Indian Reservation in an area designated as the South Unit of the Badlands National Park near the town of Interior, South Dakota.

If Crazy Horse and Black Buffalo Woman were camped there, it would have taken several days to move that far. The Stronghold is located no less than a hundred and fifty miles from Red Cloud's Agency (near present day Crawford, Nebraska).

Other detailed accounts stated,

> "The party struck north and west across the plains toward Powder River," (Bray, p. 143).

If that is true, they had quite a lengthy journey planned. It would have been two hundred miles to reach the Powder River on the closest route.

The Powder River in Wyoming starts in the Big Horn Mountains and drains north into Montana and flows into the Yellowstone River in Montana where the Crow Indians were located.

> "All day the party continued across the treeless plain dividing the Belle Fourche drainage from the Powder," (Bray, p. 143).

Bray was referring to the Belle Fourche River which starts in northeast Wyoming courses northeast and crosses the Wyoming/South Dakota line at Belle Fourche, South Dakota. That river drains east eventually into the Cheyenne River which starts in southeast Wyoming and encircles the south end of the Black Hills. The Cheyenne then flows northeast where it eventually empties into the Missouri River sixty miles north of Pierre, South Dakota.

Unless it started near Bear Butte (five miles east of Sturgis) the expedition could have taken two routes around the Black Hills. The western route would have been the closest to the Powder River Drainage. Eastern travel around the Black Hills, and not too far from the Stronghold suggested by He Dog, had many advantages.

First, water.

The Black Hills drains east. Even the south and north portions drain into streams and rivers flowing east—not into Wyoming. Rapid Creek flows east from the central Black Hills eventually emptying into the Cheyenne River. No major water flows from the Black Hills into Wyoming.

My point is that if Crazy Horse's group took the west route around the Black Hills then north toward the Powder River, they would very likely have followed the

Cheyenne River into what is now Wyoming. Leaving the Cheyenne heading north across sagebrush plains, there would have been virtually no game, except antelope. They would have had to travel at least two or three days to reach the beginning of the Belle Fourche water source.

That's risky.

If the group was truly planning to get to the Belle Fouche River drainage Bray and He Dog would have been correct.

> "The party struck north and west across the plains toward Powder River," (Bray, p. 143).

Yes, "north and west", not west and north.

Secondly, the eastern route around the Black Hills jibs with Bary's statement, "…the party continued across the treeless plain…."

Pines and deciduous trees end at the Black Hills, actually, foothills, and do not extend into the Wyoming or South Dakota "treeless" plains.

After studying many version of the Black Buffalo Woman and Crazy Horse escapade, I realized most writers have no clue about the geography, water sources, wild game availability, and distance from Red Cloud's camps or Spotted Tail's camps (near present day Chadron,

Nebraska)[17] to the camp where Crazy Horse was temporarily based.

I suggested they originally left Nebraska for the northern Black Hills and planned to camp in view of Bear Butte where water, fuel (wood) and game were available. Then they likely planned to head north toward the Belle Fourche River drainage.

It would have made sense to move toward Slim Buttes—another area known for game (especially buffalo), fuel for campfires, and security. Besides Slim Buttes was a recently claimed Lakota area which the Crow had previously cherished.

Matson, He Dog, and Bray suggest they headed at least "north."

It puzzles me why a hunting trip looking to secure buffalo meat would search anywhere close to the Red Cloud or Spotted Tail Agencies. Several thousand natives camped there. All buffalo would have been killed and eaten within two days hunter's ride from those agencies.

After the completion of the first transcontinental Union Pacific Railroad and its branch lines, the southern plains buffalo herds in Nebraska and Kansas were slaughtered. If not by railroad hunter access, by the U.S. Army and its contractors supplying buffalo meat to

---

[17] The distance between the Red Cloud Agency and Spotted Tail Agency would have been no less than forty miles.

construction crews, soldiers, agency Indians and massive caravans heading to Utah, California or Oregon.

> "In the opportunistic slaughter between 1872-1874, nearly four million buffalo were eliminated from the southern plains" (Hedren, p. 96).

There are several reason why I suggest No Water was several days ride away from his near-fatal wounding of Crazy Horse.

> "No Water tracked down Crazy Horse and Black Buffalo Woman in the Slim Buttes area."[36]

> "No Water was enraged by his wife's elopement. She and Crazy Horse had gone on a buffalo hunt in the Slim Buttes area of what is today Northwestern South Dakota."[37]

> "No Water tracked them to the Slim Buttes area of North Dakota…."[38]

All these quotes are similar, may have come from the same original source, though the last contained an error stating Slim Buttes were in North Dakota when reality is they are in South Dakota.[18]

---

[18] Quotes from Internet searches, now using Artificial Intelligence (AI) often repeat other accessible Internet material, but do not often identify their source(s) of information.

As would be expected, the jealous husband, No Water, fled the small camp immediately after shooting Crazy Horse.

> "No Water got off to a large enough lead that he was able to ride to Twin Butte…near what is today Nisland, South Dakota," (Matson, p. 68).

From a distance on the Twin Butte high vantage point, seeing Touch the Cloud and Standing Elk in pursuit, No Water rode his horse until it collapsed.

> "It died from exhaustion near the White Earth River….near what today is the community of Red Shirt Table." (Matson, p. 68-69).

William Matson reports the Clown family memories of No Water's escape. He secured a new horse and,

> "He then threw his bridle on it and rode in the direction of the Red Cloud Agency. Meanwhile, back at the hunting camp, Crazy Horse was badly hurt…, (Matson, p. 69).

Secondly, if the Crazy Horse group was going to fight Crow, it would have been no less than a week's fast travel to the closest possible Crow camps.

The distance from water supplies near Bear Butte (near present day Fort Meade, Sturgis, South Dakota) to Slim Buttes is about a hundred miles.

Distance from Slim Buttes south to Twin Buttes is about eighty miles.

If No Water rested at Twin Buttes as the Clown family reported, he would have traveled about ninety miles to Red Shirt, now a small Lakota village on the Cheyenne River just below Red Shirt Table.

In order to return to the Red Cloud Agency, No Water had to ride a new horse over a hundred miles.

In a panic on two good horses, it is possible to travel those distances--but a brutish feat for man and horse.

What we do know is No Water did not arrive on a fresh horse.

A mind-swirling jealous husband would not have lollygagged his trip to recover his wife from a known marital foe.

No Water actually may have been initially riding a mule which would have been sweaty-wet, maybe foaming at the mouth from the quick entry into camp. (Mules are known to have more stamina than horses.)

Let's address travel time.

A moving Lakota camp would have traveled between fifteen and a maximum twenty-five miles per day pulling tipis and supplies on horse drags with women tagging along.

For example, I am a distance hiker. The week I am writing this I was on two distance group hikes of thirteen miles and two days later a hike of fifteen miles. Our group of eighteen experienced hikers carrying water or only a small pack (less than five pounds) traveled at three point two miles-per-hour (3.2 mph) over a three hour period.

Less experienced hikers, or those carrying packs travel at two miles-per-hour. I would suggest that the Crazy Horse contingent would have traveled no more than two miles per hour over a ten hour day.

Granted Lakota on horses pulling drags and walking would have been in much better condition than this seventy-two-year-old. A significantly sized group moving and camping day after day would not exceed the limits suggested above.

When moving day-after-day, group movement is slow and deliberate.

Here's a personal example, I called my aunt on her ninetieth birthday in the fall of 2024 and asked her to tell me something I didn't know about her father (my grandfather). She said,

> "Did he ever tell you when he was thirteen that he and Uncle Henry (age twelve) and my grandfather couldn't afford railway fare, so they walked driving the small herd of cattle over five hundred miles from eastern Iowa to our first farm in South Dakota."[39]

"When was that," I asked.

My aunt quickly responded, "1905."

It took them two months, camping at night where there was water.

The Crazy Horse contingent would have moved at a similar speed—likely slightly farther since they were not driving cattle.

When did they eat?

Large Lakota meals were likely served in late afternoon and evening. Light quick meal of leftovers or dried meat were likely consumed in the morning.

Departure and arrival would have been based on sun and heat.

Also likely, the group, in no rush and under no duress, would have left around seven a.m., traveled with few breaks at streams to water horses, and called it a day and began setting up camp about four p.m.

Reports vary on when No Water arrived at the Crazy Horse camp. During daylight—probably late afternoon? At night after the meal?

Some writers suggested that it was late afternoon, but here's an answer that seems satisfactory.

> "It was early in the evening and our hunting party's tipis glowed with the golden warmth of inner campfires," (Matson, p. 68).

Nine hours per day at two miles per hour would have allowed the group to camp near water every fifteen to twenty miles.

If they only made it north to the Badland's Stronghold, it would have taken at least five days.

Why would buffalo hunters go into the Badlands, (almost devoid of vegetation and water) and look for buffalo meat?

Why would they leave to explore a potential fight with Crow Indians and travel five days to The Stronghold with absolutely no possibility of meeting Crow?

How many days was it between Crazy Horse and Black Buffalo Woman' contingent leaving their Nebraska's camp and No Water's arrival?

Other writers seem to suggest they traveled for two days.

I think they traveled for several days. It was likely a week to ten days based on the escape of No Water and his return to the Red Cloud Agency.

From Slim Buttes to Red Cloud Agency following the route mentioned above would have been no less than 170 miles. It would have taken the Crazy Horse group about ten days to make that trip.

Could No Water ride that distance in three days?

Yes. It is possible.

Here's why.

What was likely the longest and quickest ride recorded in the wild west was by William "Buffalo Bill" Cody.

> "…General (Philip Henry) Sheridan (1831-1888) in his Memoirs, (wrote) 'Cody road three hundred and fifty miles in less than sixty hours,'" (Wetmore, p. 157).[40]

No Water, his wife, Black Buffalo Woman, and Crazy Horse were initially in the same camp. No Water left camp to either join Red Cloud (who most likely was in Washington or at his Red Cloud Agency in northwest Nebraska), or No Water left to get alcohol from a trader (which could have been located in Nebraska, South Dakota, or possibly even closer to Fort Fetterman on the Platte River in Wyoming).

If as some claim No Water was after alcohol, he must have been on a very long binge.

For later reference, keep in mind that a trader, Joseph Larrabee (1825-1890), had a mobile trading post near Red Cloud's camp and later moved it to the Spotted Tail Agency.

Larrabee's daughter, Nellie, eventually married Crazy Horse. If No Water had been to Larabee's trading post since he was a "Hang-Around-the-Fort" person, he likely knew Nellie before Crazy Horse.

Note that Laravie may not have set up a trading post until 1873—three years after No Water shot Crazy Horse. This was based on He Dog's memory of an activity that happened fifty-seven years earlier.[41]

However, He Dog's location report seems accurate, but the date of 1873 doesn't match military records of Spotted Tails Agency which wasn't yet established and didn't move to South Dakota until October 29, 1877.

Laravie's trading post may have been near the Spotted Tail Agency (a.k.a. Camp Sheridan) before he moved it to Rosebud, South Dakota near what became the new location of the Spotted Tail Agency.

To finalize this travel review, let me just confirm:

1. Crazy Horse left with Black Buffalo Woman as his mate.
2. Touch The Cloud, Standing Elk, Black Bear, Black Bear's wife, and Black Buffalo Woman all assumed Crazy Horse was then mated to Black Buffalo Woman.
3. No Water wanted his wife back.
4. Black Buffalo Woman had not sought, and if she did, had not received a divorce from No Water according to tribal custom.

That means Crazy Horse had ample time to engage in marital activity with Black Buffalo Woman during the trip.

Considering both were in prime reproductive age, during one of many horse watering stops it would not surprise me if the two went over the hill, around the corner, and privately checked out the water and grass along the creek.

Chapter 10

What Happened?

No Water rode into camp and asked if Crazy Horse was there.

Someone said or pointed to Black Bear's tipi which confirmed there was more than one tipi.

On alert hearing the gallop into camp, Black Buffalo Woman snuck under the back side of Black Bear's tipi and likely remained quiet and hid. She knew she had to escape the tipi before her husband, No Water, appeared at the entrance flap.

No Water looked inside and pointed his borrowed pistol at Crazy Horse's heart.

The largest man in the tipi and closest to the entrance was Touch The Cloud. Upon realizing the danger, he quickly hit the pistol as No Water fired.

The bullet struck Crazy Horse in the face (some suggest near his left nostril). The bullet smashed through his jawbone and apparently exited out his neck without piercing a juggler vein.

Kingsley Bray graphically describes the incident.

> "The gun barked, scarcely a foot from Crazy Horse's face…as the bullet struck just below his left nostril, plowing a surface wound along the nine of his teeth and fracturing his upper jaw before exiting his neck at the base of the skull. (Having partially risen)…Crazy Horse took a step, then pitched forward unconscious into the cooking fire," (Bray, p. 145).

No Water, realizing he killed Crazy Horse, ran for his wet horse (or possibly mule) and made a mad dash out of camp.

Everyone was in shock.

Black Buffalo Woman remained hidden until her husband had left. After administering first aid to Crazy Horse, the men assessed what to do.

Black Bear's wife and Black Buffalo Woman stabilized Crazy Horse. Since No Water thought he had killed Crazy Horse, very likely Crazy Horse passed out. Otherwise, No Water would have surely heard screams of agony.

A plan was developed. Three men, including Standing Elk and Touch The Clouds, gathered their weapons, likely some food and water, and readied their horses to track down No Water.

Having a significant lead and likely a pre-planned exit, allowed No Water to escape into the darkness.

In the previous chapter, I covered the path of No Water's return to the Red Cloud Agency which was actually Red Cloud's camp, as his Agency had not yet been officially established.[42]

The Red Cloud's camp was an entanglement of independent subchiefs, war widows, elderly, and children of mixed relationships with hunters, scouts, and warriors coming and going in not always an organized system.

One thing is certain, it was not a shock to the camp when Crazy Horse left with Black Buffalo Woman.

Secondly, Crazy Horse was a Shirt Wearer. He was bestowed that honor by the Shirt Wearer Society in 1865 based on his braveness and response in battle and his care for the tribe.

By accepting his specifically made shirt, Crazy Horse gained additional responsibilities like other Shirt Wearers. It involved advising senior chiefs on where might be the best place to hunt, camp, and importantly offensive and defensive tribal objectives.

No Water, being in the same camp, although older than Crazy horse, had not received special status as a Shirt Wearer.

Black Buffalo Woman likely saw more opportunity courting the younger and apparently more daring Crazy Horse. However, she had mothering responsibilities having fathered No Water's daughters.

If Red Cloud's camp had animosity conflicts before No Water shot Crazy Horse, those issues magnified upon No Water's return.

Worm (if you remember was Crazy Horse's father) apparently left the Red Cloud camp to attend to his son—if he was still living.

Similarly, years later when Crazy Horse was actually killed September 5, 1877, Worm also responded immediately. He held his son into the evening until Crazy Horse died. (More on the second incident later.)

One version (Bray) wrote that Crazy Horse was taken to the camp of his uncle, Spotted Crow.

Complex negotiations resulted to keep tribal unity because of violations of tribal customs.

Though I find no reference to No Water, Black Buffalo Woman, Worm, or Crazy Horse being exposed to the Bible through missionaries, tribal response leaves no doubt they all subscribed to at least four of the Commandments (5th don't kill, 6th don't commit adultery;

8th be kind to others; and 10th don't covet someone's wife).[43]

No Water had expressed earlier dissatisfaction with Crazy Horse flirting with his wife.

He Dog, in his interviews, assumed Crazy Horse accepted Black Buffalo Woman as his wife which implied a consensual sexual relationship, (Bray, p. 144). Since no family, community, or tribal consent had been given to Black Buffalo Woman's right of divorce, she therefore was still considered married to No Water.

By requesting a pistol before leaving camp, No Water intended to kill Crazy Horse.

In the various scenarios No Water, Black Buffalo Woman, Crazy Horse, Worm, Red Cloud, and Spotted Tail were all involved in resolution of the incident.

Negotiations began immediately likely absent of Red Cloud who may still have been on a Washington trip.

Crazy Horse did not want Black Buffalo Woman punished for her indiscretion. To put a stop to the internal bickering, Crazy Horse gave up his claim to Black Buffalo Woman.

No Water, and their tribe complied. She went back to being the wife of No Water (although some time likely had elapsed). It must have been well before she gave birth to her third (possibly forth) daughter.

Tribal drama and negotiation have been described in detail by other authors, (Bray, pp. 145-147; Matson, pp. 69-70; Sajna, pp. 158-159, 226-229).

Although Worm had arrived to take care of his son, he was there for two apparent reasons, emotional support and seek healing of Crazy Horse's wound.

Tribal unity had deteriorated.

Since long-term care was needed, and it was prudent to keep Crazy Horse from No Water, it is likely that Worm sought the help of Spotted Tail, an uncle of Crazy Horse.

Spotted Tail was a Sicangu (a.k.a. Brule) Lakota. Whereas Red Cloud, an Oglala Lakota, and his protégé, No Water, were in a different camp.

In another incident after Crazy Horse had healed from a shot in the mouth, they were both hunting buffalo near the Big Horn River. No Water was given Moccasin Top's horse to escape as Crazy Horse was arriving. Sajna stated,

> "Afterwards, No Water traveled south to join the loafer Indians[19] at the Red Cloud Agency," (Sajna, p. 228)

---

[19] "Loafer Indians" and "Hang-Around-the-Fort-Indians" were interchangeable derogatory terms used by non-Progressive Lakota that supported the freedom Crazy Horse desired.

That statemen is another confirmation that No Water, and his regained wife, Black Buffalo Woman, remained in Red Cloud's camp which was near present day Henry, Nebraska very near the Wyoming border (about nine miles southeast of Torrington, Wyoming).

Spotted Tail exhibited his responsibility and deserved respect for his diplomacy by offering his niece, Black Shaw, as personal nurse to care for Crazy Horse's healing.

A more contentious head chief would have taken different action. For example,

> "(In) 1838, a man from Broken Bow's camp stole a wife from another camp. This caused bad feelings and the man was killed," (Sneve, p. 21).

Tempers had flared on both sides. No Water and Crazy Horse supporters were ready to fight. Red Cloud and Spotted Tail's camps were in an uproar while Red Cloud was in Washington.

Thanks to wise man Spotted Tail, No Water regained his wife, Crazy Horse left them alone, and Black Shaw, shortly thereafter, became the first, and longest serving wife of Crazy Horse.

Chapter 11

The Healer

Black Shawl was twenty-five and had never been married. Five years younger than Crazy Horse added benefits to the relationship.

> First, "...Black Shawl had proven herself to be a good at healing bullet wounds," (Matson, p. 69).

With all the conflicts before and after the incident with No Water, Crazy Horse was likely looking for someone that could care for his inflictions.

Bonus.

Black Shawl was obviously well acquainted with gathering and mixing various herbs for healing. Food preparation, ability to organize tipi construction and dismantling, and other Brule camp responsibilities made her a life-mate for Crazy Horse.

They apparently married within a month of meeting as Crazy Horse's jaw wound had not completely healed. At first, the timing sounded strange.

Quick romance?

Healing from wounds by a bullet fired by a angry husband to marrying the nurse seems implausible in today's timeline of courting.

Consider who we are addressing—Crazy Horse.

At thirty years old, and daring life on the wild plains, what it quick?

During WWI and WWII soldiers home on leave married a previously unknown sweetheart during the two week romance. Perhaps more surprising to some is that soldiers in the Atlantic and Pacific theaters, brought home "War Brides" that had served them a few beers during RR (rest and relaxation).

Wars cause wounds. More people are injured and survive wars than are killed. It was more common to assign soldiers to a area for convalescence, than to give them a medical discharge. Many times, after healing, they went back to battle.

Single nurses serving in Red Cross hospitals treating wounded soldiers often developed a relationship that resulted in marriage. A popular Red Cross service was to hand out coffee and donuts to troops.

In fact, U.S. immigration policy changed quickly under the 1945 War Bride's Act based on the overwhelming number of servicemen returning with their wife or fiancé.[44]

Consequently, it does not surprise me that Black Shawl quickly found a person she could help and love.

Remember, Crazy Horse had returned from a conflict with Crow and was likely looking to scout other potential Crow intrusion while on his buffalo hunt with Black Buffalo Woman.

It was war time.

Relationships do not wait for war to end. During wars, nobody knows when it will end. Why wait to marry?

Depending on the source, stories vary as to relationship between Crazy Horse and Black Shawl. I contend it was consensual.

She was not described as beautiful. Instead she had a beautiful heart.

> "She had a plain face, an average build, and a beautiful heart," (Matson, p. 70).

Crazy Horse would have known he had a permanent, disfiguring facial wound. Lesser brave men would have been self-conscious and been forever shy of women. Not Crazy Horse.

Was he looking for a wife? Yes.

Otherwise, he would not have run away with Black Buffalo Woman.

In her mid-twenties, Crazy Horse found a perfect mate. She cared for him despite his looks. Black Shawl cared for him when he couldn't care for himself. She cared for him knowing his immediate history with another women and a future when he would be away from home.

Lakota were known as consuming "dry cooked" foods. As nomadic, that meant they ate meat cooked over an open fire. Sioux counterparts in eastern South Dakota and Minnesota had semi-permanent settlements and used "wet cooking" methods.

When moving all the time, cooking pottery would have broken bouncing on a pony drags over rocks and holes, mile after mile, day after day. Practicalities of Lakota life required minimum baggage, cookware, and tools when traveling.

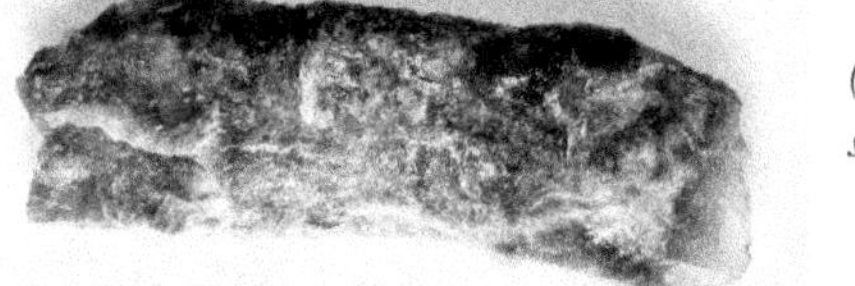

(Photo Gary Wietgrefe collection small four inch flint knife.)

With a hole in his mouth and jaw, and likely a neck muscle damaged, could Crazy Horse eat buffalo jerky?

No.

Black Shawl no doubt made liquid foods for him.

Some authors mentioned Black Shawl fed Crazy Horse through a straw.

That's crazy!

Holding your head, mouth and jaw in one position would have been painful. How uncaring would it have been if Black Shawl brought in a watery gruel and said, "I made a meal. Here's a straw. Suck this down."

Though hungry he would have winced at the thought.

He obviously couldn't chew, nor suck on a straw. A very athletic thirty-year-old man living on mainly protein, Black Shawl must have baby-spoon fed him constantly for many days to maintain his strength while healing took place.

Brule and Lakota women were known to be very quiet when men were in camp unless separated and gossiping with their fellow wives, relatives, or friends. Mostly timid, they didn't seek recognition and were far more caring than their reactive husbands.

Do doubt, Black Shawl was the perfect wife. She healed Crazy Horse in his most desperate moment (shot by his lover's husband).

What a wife!

In the days to come, she would have prepared food for his travels, cut and mended his clothes, organized their tipi, and loaded their pony drag for the next move.

A bonus--genetically, they were not related.

Intimacy followed.

The following year, 1871, Black Shawl gave birth to Crazy Horse's only claimed child, They Are Afraid of Her. Her name was the repeated family name of his maternal aunt.

Black Shawl raised They Are Afraid of Her mostly by herself, but the baby was not neglected by her father. War is a tough thing. It separated husbands and wives, brothers and sisters, fathers and children.

While Crazy Horse had not completely healed, his younger half-brother, Little Hawk, was killed in western Nebraska by Shoshone (Sajna, p. 228). However, the Shoshone were known to control an area in the Big Horn Mountains in west-central Wyoming. It is more likely Lakota had transgressed into Shoshone country searching for buffalo and disturbing white migration west.

Not one to lay around or slow to make decisions, Crazy Horse felt the urge to take revenge against the Shoshone and take what they could from any whites.

Apparently, on his trip into Wyoming that is where Crazy Horse first met Sitting Bull. Conjoined with the same thoughts of saving Lakota land and roaming culture, the two crossed paths often and conspired.

Otherwise, how could they have pulled off the most dramatic and successful coordinated Battle of the Little Bighorn where Lieutenant Colonel Custer and his Seventh Calvary were utterly destroyed?

It wasn't just Crazy Horse and Sitting Bull in the fight. Many may not know that Hump, Two Eagles, Gall and many other chiefs of other Lakota Sioux, Arapaho, and Northern Cheyenne tribes coordinated the successful attack on Custer's troops.

Another caveat is that the Battle of Little Bighorn took place on a Montana Crow Indian Reservation that was established in 1868—eight years after Crow's Reservation had been established.

This background is presented to give readers an idea of the massive area Crazy Horse covered after he was nearly killed by No Water. From western Nebraska, south to north across the eastern half of Wyoming into southwest Montana and the western half of South Dakota was where Crazy Horse maneuvered.

Now, relate to Black Shawl.

She had to raise a child mostly by herself. Secure and preserve food were mandatory when time allowed. On a moment's notice she had to treat his injuries and always have preparations ready when, and if, her husband returned.

Again, what a woman!

Chapter 12

Cost of Cause

Remember Crazy Horse was a member of the Lakota Shirt Wearer Society?

That was to be a permanent responsibility. Shirt Wearers were tested, quizzed and deemed responsible enough to advise tribal leaders.

The studious Yankton Sioux writer, Ella Cara Deloria (1889-1971), explained the importance of the men's council.

> "The council was the central institution for the expression of Lakota wisdom and virtue…(and included) only those of 'mature judgement'…" (Albers, p. 242).[45]

With the shirt came not only respect but expectations.

Affair with a colleague's wife was not one of them.

Would Crazy Horse have to give his shirt back?

If so, to whom?

Should No Water get it?

Tribal chiefs needed responsible, field-tested advisors. It wasn't that they could just put names in a moccasin and draw another shirt wearer.

While tempers of revenge were flaming between No Water and Crazy Horse supporters, Red Cloud, Spotted Tail and subchiefs had to take action before intra-tribal conflict destroyed their ability to fight others.

After much consultation, it was decided Crazy Horse would have to permanently give up his coveted Shirt. It was never awarded to anyone again.

> "Crazy Horse could not be a 'shirt-wearer' any more on account of his adultery."[46]

Another account,

> "...(is) the issue of Crazy Horse's adultery. It came to an inevitable conclusion: Crazy Horse had made himself unworthy of his status as a Shirt Wearer..." (Bray, p. 147).

Honor from being a Shirt Wearer was lost. Counseling 'Chiefs of staff" ended. Just like in the military, if generals lose respect for a lower-ranking lieutenant, colonel, or major their advice is dismissed—no matter how valid.

Did Crazy Horse then shirk his responsibilities as a Lakota warrior?

Absolutely not.

No Water, for deliberately requesting a pistol under false pretenses and shooting a fellow warrior, he had to give up something as punishment.

What?

Not a Shirt?

No.

Horses.

Since the time Sioux moved west out of Wisconsin and Minnesota, horses were the most valuable trade item. Wives were acquired by giving her father horses. Unless horses were stolen, like Crazy Horse's father, buffalo meat, hides, furs, guns, ammunition, and alcohol were traded for brides.

No Water negotiated to settle his shot at Crazy Horse by giving him two horses, a roan and bay (Sajna, p. 227).

In return, at the demand by Crazy Horse, No Water would get his wife, Black Buffalo Woman, back if he agreed to not punish her, not disfigure her, and never again be known to mistreat her.

Since negotiations were handled (by necessity) quickly, not too much time had elapsed between No

Water shooting Crazy Horse and Black Buffalo Woman's return as (conjecture has it) a pregnant wife.

Readers, please do not assume raging animosity between the two men had been settled. It wasn't.

Although both men were generally guided under Red Clouds protectorate, Crazy Horse and No Water avoided overnighting in the same camps.

Another cost of cause was that Crazy Horse was not allowed any association with Black Buffalo Woman. If he had a child from her, he likely never met the child.

Not all was lost.

Crazy Horse gained two half-brothers, Iron Horse (about his age), and Red Feather Black Shawl's younger brother.

Although information is sketchy, it appears that all three got along well. Red Feather, while idolizing Crazy Horse as a fierce independent warrior, was cautious to protect his sister.

Red Feather obviously could not help from being constantly reminded of the affair with Black Buffalo Woman each time he looked at Crazy Horse's facial wound.

Just as a sidenote, Crazy Horse apparently painted a prominent lightning strike from his nose across his left jaw unto his neck to camouflage his self-consciousness and emphasize his warrior appearance.

Again, to emphasize the closeness of Black Shawl and Crazy Horse, he scheduled to be in camp when his daughter, They Are Afraid of Her, was delivered.

Finally, after tragically losing his mother, his brother and nearly losing his life to a shot in the head, Crazy Horse swooned over his young daughter. She became the love of his life.

In troubled times, life can be short.

His tender girl, They Are Afraid of Her, died of cholera a couple years later, 1873.

Cholera is usually contracted by drinking contaminated water. Lakota settlements were not permanent. When forced to live near water sources for long periods, runoff from human waste, animal offal, feces, and other decay likely infected drinking water.

Crazy Horse was operating in a world-view vacuum.

He had never been to Washington, D.C. like Red Cloud who had traveled by rail to meet President Ulysses S. Grant, senators, and East Coast businessman in 1870.

It is likely Red Cloud was on his east coast peace tour during the Crazy Horse--Black Buffalo Woman affair.

Unconnected to mail service, telegraph, and newspapers (being illiterate), Crazy Horse could not comprehend the world beyond Lakota territory occupied or captured since he was a young boy.

By 1851, when Crazy Horse was eleven, Lakota had quite successfully driven other tribes from western South Dakota, northern Nebraska and eastern Wyoming.

That same year the Treaty of Traverse des Sioux was a coerced agreement between the U.S. government in cooperation with Alexander Ramsey, Governor of Minnesota Territory who acquired, through treaty, Sisseton and Wahpeton Sioux land by cession.

Tribes communicated. No doubt Crazy Horse had heard stories of how other Sioux Tribes had to give up their land because buffalo were gone. Fellow tribespeople in Minnesota and eastern South Dakota were basically starved into treaty submission.

This important childhood memory would have been a valuable lesson for Crazy Horse's future location of his own reservation.

Crazy Horse traveled a lot, but I cannot speculate on what he knew or did not know about specific battles or raids.

Here are a few events upon which Crazy Horse likely contemplated. Lacking communications with the white world would have limited his knowledge.

- End U.S. Civil War in 1865. Thereafter, many more Army soldiers moved into Lakota territory.

- Dakota Sioux War August 1862 in western Minnesota.
- Fetterman Massacre December 1866 (southern Wyoming).
- Transcontinental Union Pacific Railroad, 1863-1869 through Sioux territory in Nebraska.
- Equine influenza of 1872.
- Worldwide economic panic of 1873 lasted through 1877 causing investment bank insolvency, collapse of international businesses, railroad labor strikes, and bankruptcies including the construction pause of Northern Pacific Railroad through northern Sioux territory.
- Custer's Expedition July 2 through August 30, 1874, through the Black Hills of South Dakota (coveted newly claimed Lakota territory) where gold was reportedly discovered.
- Fort Abraham Lincoln attached by Sioux May 1873 south of Mandan, North Dakota.
- Red Cloud, Spotted Tail, and Lone Horn traveled to Washington, D.C. May 1875.
- Great Sioux War (1876-1877) known as the battle for the Black Hills.
- Battle of Powder River, March 1876 (Montana Territory).
- Battle of Rosebud June 1876 (Montana Territory);
- Battle of Little Bighorn June 1876 (Montana Territory).

- Battle of Slim Buttes, September 1876 (northwest South Dakota).
- Battle of Cedar Creek, October 1876, (Montana Territory); and
- Battle of Muddy Creek, May 1877 (Montana Territory).

Major things that occurred in the U.S. during Crazy Horse's short life were mostly beyond his control. Others, he acted as a young decoy (Fetterman Massacre), joined with other forces (Battle of Little Bighorn), or conducted the main operation (Battle of Slim Buttes).

No wonder he needed a wife that could care for wounds and have camp affairs in order when he arrived.

Black Shawl had her own sickness to deal with—tuberculosis. She had been sick for a long time. Sometimes Crazy Horse was with her, often not.

On May 7th, 1877, Crazy Horse was with her when Doctor Valentine T. McGillycuddy, an Army contract doctor, was called to look at Black Shawl.

> "…McGillycuddy visited the village and attended Crazy Horse's tipi at the war chief's request to examine Black Shawl," (Bray, p. 297).

With his wife sick, likely unable to care for herself, Crazy Horse, needed help—not only to care for his wife, his tipi, but also to prepare him for his future.

Soon he married wife two—Nellie Larrabee.

Chapter 13

Behind Brown Eyes

What name shall I use? Ista Gli Win or in English "Brown Eyes Woman" is the Lakota name for Helena, Helen, Ellen, or Nellie Larrabee, Larribee, Laribee, Laravie, Larvie, and probably some other spellings.

The second wife of Crazy Horse I will call Nellie which seems like the most commonly used at the time.

Nellie's father, Joseph Larrabee (1825-1890), was a Frenchman born in St. Charles in the far southeast part of Missouri. As a young man he most likely hired on with nearby Missouri River boats hauling supplies to the upper reaches of that river and its tributaries.

Although his French/English was pronounced with a southern drawl, he obviously had a gift for understanding and speaking Indian languages used in trading up-river boat supplies in exchange for Plains hides (deer, antelope, elk and buffalo) and pelts (fox, coyote, otter, mink, skunk, muskrat, beaver, wolf and bear).

Pronunciations even of his surname was not always understood. Known as a French fur trader, Joe, traded in several states for the American Fur Trading Company. He had to be illiterate.

Considering "R" is vibrated from the back of the mouth in French compared to the clearer "R" sound from folded front tongue in English and "B" puffed out and "V" oft said with an "OU" sound, many heard his name differently. Larrabee to some sounded like Laravie to others. Given elimination of southern drawl in northern English, Joe's trade records were likely written as Larvie.

(In no references have I seen where Joe used the surname spelling of his French grandfather L'Arrivee.)

One reference stated:

> "The French voyageur, Joseph Larabee…once worked for the Hudson Bay Company," (Lee, p. 116).[47]

As a fur trader, most assuredly Joe worked nearly exclusively for or with John Jacob Astor's American Fur Trading Company.[20]

---

[20] American Fur Trading Company had nearly a monopoly on the fur and hide trade in the Dakotas and Minnesota Territories in 1840s to 1860s.

"Trade," often at a rendezvous, was conducted at semi-permanent exchange locations, preferably located near a water shipping port. Later, "trading posts" were located inland to deliver everything from coffee and salt to guns, alcohol and ammunition to Indians in exchange for pelts and buffalo hides.

Fur trading meant that traders, like Larrabee, never actually trapped but instead received animal pelts[21] from Indians during late fall to late winter harvests when animals had their winter coats.

Money was of no value on the Plains. Trade was done without money. The wealthy John Jacob Astor[22] an Englishman of German decent became a very wealthy American that converted furs to money. Perhaps Joseph "Joe" Larrabee made an exchange gaining a Northern Cheyenne Indian wife, called Chi Chi.

In case you are trying to track down a family with various surname spellings, depending on location, Joe was also called "Long John."

Chi Chi bore four daughter from Joe. Julia (1850-1909), Sarah (1851-1937), Helen "Nellie" (1853-1928), Elizabeth (1854-1910). Birth years may be quite accurate

---

[21] Pelts are animal skins, whereas furs have been conditioned (generally cleaned and salted) to preserve the furs for outbound shipment.

[22] John Jacob Astor (1864-1912), the most famous person that died on the Titanic was named after his grandfather, John Jacob Astor, the original fur trader.

but they certainly do not match the many degrading references to Nellie as Crazy Horse's *teenage* wife.[48]

Just for reference, Nellie was likely only two years old when her mother died. This is interesting because Crazy Horse tragically lost his mother when he was four.

No doubt with four young daughters to care for, Nellie's father, Joe, remarried shortly after her death.

Nellie's stepmother, Mary Elizabeth Metcalf-Larvie, apparently helped move the family from the Cheyenne River area in South Dakota to Montana where Alexander was born in 1855 or 1856.

Joe's second wife, Mary, produced boys and was likely pregnant when the "Long John" trader Joe moved from Montana to Nebraska where Philip and sister Zoe (likely twins) were born in 1858.

Likely, young Nellie and her sisters were busy caring for their baby brothers, because William was born in 1860. After a move to eastern Wyoming to another trading post in northeast Colorado where Thomas was born in 1863. He was followed by Rose in 1870.

Nellie was about seventeen when brother Joseph (1871) was born followed by Richard who was born in 1876 when their dad, Joe, moved his trading post to what became the Rosebud Reservation in South Dakota.

By then food and cooking supplies, cloth, wagons, wheels, blacksmithing tools, horse harnesses, and tack supplemented the nearly non-existent access to pelts. New buffalo hides to purchase didn't exist then in northwest Nebraska and southern South Dakota.

What buffalo remained in northwest South Dakota were harvested for hide and tongue and shipped down the Missouri River.

As the fur trade tapered out, traders switched to accumulating buffalo hides which were transported as back-hauls on freight wagons to settlements on railroads.

Any place in the world, throughout history, merchants, often traders, were a critical link of commerce.

Just like Joe Larrabee connected the Cheyenne Indians in South Dakota to American goods from the eastern states and Canada, he did the same for Crows in Montana, and Lakota in Wyoming, Nebraska and South Dakota.

This may seem like a sidetrack from Nellie, Crazy Horse's second wife. I believe it was why the wise, and thoughtful Crazy Horse sought her.

Before I go there, I'll mention I made a living in agriculture as a professional agronomist with a keen interest in millets of which I've written a couple books.

I contend that proso millet (used for grain, food, and straw for forage), and the most drought-hardy grain, should have been introduced to Lakota reservations when the government tried to get them to farm in the 1870s.

German-Russians pioneers, after 1880, seeded proso (a short-season ancient food grain) in rotation with wheat (for flour) and oats (for horses).

Currently ninety percent of U.S. proso millet is grown in the Rosebud Sioux Reservation in Millette and Todd Counties of South Dakota through the area of Red Cloud and Spotted Tail's permanent camps in Nebraska and production ends in far northeast Colorado—the southwest area of Lakota one-time territory.

Proso millet had been connected as a food and trading item for thousands of years. The high protein, nutritious grain, proso, originated in northern China ten thousand years ago and was transported by horses from the time of the Persian Empire (500 B.C.) though central Asia into Europe.

The Persian Empire is ancient history. There is evidence, however, native peoples lived in western South Dakota 5,000 years before the Persian Empire.

> "The oldest Indian site found in western South Dakota is in the Angostura Basin south of Hot Springs. Studies indicate it to be a little more than 7,000 years old…(where) people were big-game hunters…."[49]

Several times I have mentioned horses allowed the Lakota to roam west. From the late 1700s to the surrender of Crazy Horse in 1877 they had a nomadic culture. At most, it lasted a century in western South Dakota.

From dogs, as their only beast of burden in Minnesota, Lakota transitioned to pony drags and buffalo hunters on horses.

Wild horses had to be trained. That is likely how Crazy Horse's grandfather first got the name.

Skill to ride a wild horse likely became the name Crazy Horse.

Where and when did the Lakota get horses?

> "During the 18th century, parties of Arikara from the Missouri River went on buffalo hunts as far west as the Black Hills. There they met with the Comanche, Arapaho, Kiowa, and Cheyenne at trading fairs where they acquired horses. The Arikara, in turn, traded horses with the Teton Sioux who had been slowly migrating south and westward since about 1670 from the headwaters of the Mississippi River. Around 1775 the Oglala and Brule, tribes of the Teton Sioux, moved west of the Missouri River to occupy respectively the Bad River country around the present town of Philip South Dakota…" (Badlands, Cultural Heritage Center[50]).

Horses meant wealth.

Horses were used in trade for brides. For example, Crazy Horses mother, Rattling Blanket Woman, required a dowry of eight horses.

Hores also allowed faster communication between Lakota settlements.

After horses became readily available, they were trained, used for transport, traded, sped communications, were food, and used for mobile fighting.

One more story about Nellie's father. He liked horses. When living on the Rosebud Reservation, he owned the land including hot springs (now Hot Springs) South Dakota. Lakota called it the place of *Mni khata* or translated *Minnekahata* meaning "hot water."

> "In the fall of 1879 Joseph Laravie, a Frenchman, with a squaw wife, came from the Reservation to bath at the famous Minnekahta, and built a cabin over the spring as a protection…."[51]

The following year with the help of a Mr. Turner and Mr. John Davidson for the Pine Ridge Agency, Laravie built a seventy-feet-long log hotel there.

Joe liked horses. Apparently he sold the hot springs property to purchase a fast horse for a one-on-one race on the Nebraska/South Dakota border area. It was apparently near Whiteclay, Nebraska where Reservation Indians to this day buy beer and take it onto the Pine Ridge Reservation which bans alcohol.

Joe sold the Hot Springs property for $600.00 and a very fast Thoroughbred gray stallion. (Lee & Williams, p. 159).[52]

Bets from businessmen, ranchers and Indians quickly became a big deal. Though controversial, Lakotans on the South Dakota side won the pot of money and quickly crossed into South Dakota where they could not be contested.

Crazy Horse, like his fellow chiefs, wanted fast horses used in battles, during hunting, and communications. They followed a very old tradition.

Greek historian, Herodotus (484-425 BC) wrote about horses by stating, "Nothing in the world travels faster than the Persian couriers." Where do you think the U.S. Postal Service got the pre-telegraph idea of the (1860-1861) Pony Express?

This family background about Nellie is provided to give readers a clue as to the experiences she brought to the marriage. What was behind those well-traveled, well connected Brown Eyes?

Besides companionship after he surrendered at Fort Robinson Nebraska May 6, 1877, what could Nellie offer Crazy Horse?

Chapter 14

Relationships

Nellie and Crazy Horse had a lot in common.

- They both lost mothers between the ages of two and four.
- She had experience caring for others (her younger brothers and sisters).
- He had need for someone to take care of his ailing wife, Black Shawl.
- They both had lived (or camped) and traveled in Nebraska, South Dakota, Montana, and Wyoming.
- She had experience inventorying trading post supplies. That would be a critical need if he was to get his own agency.
- They both had lighter skin.
- They both had experiences with the Northern Cheyenne (her mother's tribe), Brule and Oglala Lakota, and the perpetual enemy Crow (from her

living in Montana where her younger brother was born).

- Crazy Horse had to seek rations for his followers while she had experience using white man's allocated rations.

With limited rations, each food item had to be put to use. Unfortunately, Lakota women were not trained on how to cook with what was allocated. More on this topic will be covered later.

Nellie (1953-1928) gave Crazy Horse a raft of younger brothers (really brothers-in-law). Plus, Nellie's older sister, Sarah (1851-1937), had been eyeing an up-and-coming bullwhacker and future cattleman, James "Scotty" Philip (1858-1911)—a potential brother-in-law by marriage.

> "Sarah's father, Joseph Laribee (1825-1935), was respected by many who knew of his exploits among the tribes westward to the Rockies. Through the wilderness he had lived among the Cheyennes, Crows, Snakes, and Blackfeet. His dealings…allowed him to give subsidized help to Scotty in his early freighting and stock-raising ventures," (Robinson, p. 61). [53]

Nellie's oldest sister, Julia (1850-1909), married Michael Dunn (1845-1921), a Civil War veteran. They made their home in Stanley County, South Dakota. Michael and Julia became large cattle ranchers and were regular friends and visitors to Scotty and Sarah Philip's ranch.

Her sister Elizabeth (1854-1910) married Henry Lafferty (1852-1934) on April 2, 1877, which was a month before Crazy Horse surrendered. They made their home near Dupree, South Dakota.

Alexander (1856-1917) was Nellie's oldest brother. He married Mollie Anne Black Crow-Gerry (1868-1935).[23] They had eight children and made their home in Mellette County, South Dakota.[54]

Sister, Zoe (1858-1950), married James E. "Cornie" Utterback (1853-1939). As a successful cattle rancher, they were often guests of Scotty and Sarah Philips.

Cornie Utterback's initial trade was as a blacksmith at Fort Robinson. While there, Utterback was an eyewitness to the stabbing of Crazy Horse. He later became a blacksmith at Fort Pierre, South Dakota.

Utterbacks are buried in the quaint little Cedar Hill Cemetery overlooking the Bad River just outside (west) of Fort Pierre, South Dakota.

---

[23] Mollie Black Crow-Gerry's father, Elbridge Gerry III (1818-1875), was a rather famous trader and horseman who had at least six Lakota, Cheyenne, and Arikara wives and was a great-grandnephew of Elbridge signer of the Declaration of Independence and the U.S. Vice President under James Madison (1813-1814).

Philip Larrabee (1858-1945) is one of Nellie's younger brothers born after her father Joseph married Mary Elizabeth Metcalf (1840-1898). Philip is buried in Millette County, and his wife, Mary Hill (1862-1955) was laid to rest in Todd County, South Dakota.

William (1860-1950) was a younger brother of Nellie. He passed away at age ninety in 1950. He married Alice Ecoffey (1868-1941) who preceded him in death. They are buried in Bennette County, South Dakota.

Thomas (1863-1943) had a son Thomas and was Nellie's third youngest brother. He married Julia Crow Head (1865-1935) whose father was Crow Head (1833-1918) and her mother was Good Dog (1835-??). They were laid to rest in Millette County, South Dakota.

Rose (1868-1935), Nellie's youngest sister, married William "Bill" Gerry (1863-1928) an Army private and Indian scout who is buried in Hot Springs, South Dakota National Cemetery. William was a sister to Nellie's brother (Alexander's) wife, Mollie Black Crow-Gerry. Rose is buried at Saint Frances, Todd County, South Dakota.

Nellie's second to youngest brother, Joseph (1871-1921) was named after their father and may not have married. He is buried in Todd County, South Dakota.

Richard (1876-1950) was Nellie's youngest brother and Crazy Horse's youngest brother-in-law. Richard also passed away in 1950. His nickname was "Kee-Ga-Lar."

For many readers, it may be hard to believe Crazy Horse's brothers-in-law lived until 1950 when 90% of the U.S. households had television.

Richard married Addie McLean (1888-1960) whose father was James McLean (1888-1960) and her mother was Mary Stands Alone (1858-1939). They had seven children. Both Richard and his wife are buried in St. Francis, South Dakota cemeteries in Todd County, South Dakota.

Scotty Philip initially supplied hay and beef cattle needed to fill Army and Indian Agency rations. His biggest accomplishment would have made Crazy Horse smile—restoration of the buffalo. (More details later.)

Had he lived, Crazy Horse, would have had a full host of Nellie's sisters, brothers, brothers-in-law, sisters-in-law, nieces and nephews.

It is known that Joseph Larrabee, Nellie's father, gave several head of cattle to Sarah and Scotty Philips when they married in 1879.

It appears Nellie's father was a well-to-do trader and rancher.

> "Scotty had more cattle than before the wedding because his father-in-law, Joseph Larabee, had given him several head. Larabee had done well and had a big herd," (Lee, p. 118).

Earlier, as a trader, Joseph Larrabee welcomed Crazy Horse into his family and it seems he would have provided support for the independent-minded Crazy Horse.

Nellie had many young siblings. Brother Richard was only two years old when Crazy Horse was killed. Having lost is own daughter at about age three, Crazy Horse was likely enthralled with Nellie's sister Rose who would have been three years old the summer they married.

Crazy Horse's paternal grandmother is another woman hidden amongst the many forgotten women. She would have been Worm's mother.

A decade after Crazy Horse was killed, Rosebud Agency 1887 Census recorded, "Crazy Horse's Mother" age 90 born circa 1798.

She was a Lakota lady that should have been interviewed. What stories she could tell.

Chapter 15

Surrender to Black Shawl

Since the Battle of Little Bighorn (June 25, 1876), Crazy Horse and his followers had been constantly on the run from the U.S. Army. By 1877 buffalo were basically gone in much of the Plains. His followers were starving. Black Shawl was sick.

To help readers, timeline is important. A lot can happen in the very few months after Sitting Bull entered Canada with 5,000 followers—winter 1876-1877. Key events for Crazy Horse includes:

- Starving—winter 1876 into spring 1877;
- Wife unable to care for herself—April 1877;
- Multi-state travel—April-May 1877;
- Arrive at Red Cloud Agency—May 5, 1877;
- Surrender at Fort Robinson, NE—May 6, 1877;
- Food allocations—May 1877;
- Wife gets white doctor;
- Becoming a U.S. Army soldier;

- A practical romance—June 1877;
- Marries second wife—July 1877;
- Initiate a new reservation—July 1877;
- Plan a trip to Washington—August 1877;
- Killed—September 5, 1877.

In the summer of 1877 Crazy Horse and his wives lived in a prairie whirlwind.

Like the summer before (before the Battle of Little Bighorn), food was needed.

The young nephew of Crazy Horse, Red Fox, recalled community desperation.

> "On June 8, 1876, the great medicine man and prophet Sitting Bull called a council of the Sioux and Cheyenne chiefs. Among those who attended were Crazy Horse and my father Black Eagle of the Sioux and Two Moons of the Cheyennes. Sitting Bull asked, 'Shall we die of hunger and our children want for clothing from the hides of the buffalo?'" (Red Fox, p. 43).[55]

During the grueling trek along the Belle Fourche River, past Bear Butte, around the Black Hills south to northwest Nebraska, Crazy Horse accumulated a rag-tag group of nearly nine hundred, while Black Shawl was monitored by "kinswomen."[24]

---

[24] Kinswoman in a tribal sense could be her mother, grandmothers, sisters, cousins, aunts, and even close friends.

The year before surrendering (1876) searching for buffalo, elk, deer, and bear the large contingent of Sioux and Cheyenne headed into Montana. Red Fox recalled,

> "At the time I was six years old, but even today after 500 moons have passed, I can remember the long, hot dusty journey with scores of ponies struggling over the parched land dragging our tepees and other supplies," (Red Fox, p. 44).

The surrender trip (April to early May 1877) from Montana to Nebraska would have been just as bad. In those conditions, can you imagine the tasks of women trying to keep food from getting dusty?

Can you imagine struggles of women trying to clean the hair, face and clothes of children before putting them down to sleep on hard ground?

Can you imagine Black Shawl being deathly sick, struggling to breath while blocking the dusty air?

As a concerned husband, Crazy Horse comforted Black Shawl. His care for her likely led to his death—four months hence.

On the dusty trail to Fort Robinson, miners and hunters desperate for meat surely would have eliminated wild game the prior three years since discovery of gold in the Black Hills.

The group trudged south.

They arrived.

There was plenty to do. First, all were fed. Rations allocated. Day-to-day feeding his followers was removed from his plate. Instead, future plans had to be quickly laid.

Nellie Larrabee fit his plan.

Obstacle—she had other suitors.

With all the Army soldiers hanging around the fort, bullwhacker teams arriving, unloading and hanging around, Lakota, Arapaho, and Cheyenne married and unmarried men looking for something to do, eligible women were in short supply.

In their early twenties, unmarried daughters of a Cheyenne woman and a Frenchman running a nearby trading post were cherries ready for picking.

When Crazy Horse arrived, some of the Larrabee girls were single under the watchful eye of a Cheyenne mother and French Catholic father.

Not just anyone was suitable. The trading post needed workers and the girls didn't have to be paid a wage. Besides, they had a baseball team of younger brothers and sisters to care for.

Nellie was the third oldest.

Local rumors were that the single U.S. Army Lieutenant William Philo Clark (1845-1884) was after Nellie. Without getting into detail about the killing of

Crazy Horse, Lieutenant Clark was involved in his arrest, travel approval, and death.[25]

By tradition, Lakota had one name and were not yet accustomed to calling someone by first and last name. Hence, Lieutenant Clark was called "White Hat Clark."

Likely, Mr. and Mrs. Larrabee thought Clark would be a good catch for one of their daughters, but everyone carries baggage. Clark may have been too anti-Indian.

As would be expected, Nellie found interest from a young man that had been around Fort Robinson for some time. He, like many others that agreed to have peace with whites well before Crazy Horse arrived, a Hang-Around-The-Fort guy called Little Bear and nicknamed Sioux Bob had been courting Nellie.

According to author, Kingsley Bray, Sioux Bob had been serious enough about marrying Nellie that by the spring of 1877 he had already delivered pre-marital gifts to the Larrabees.

Since the Larrabees accepted his gifts, Sioux Bob, likely had the wedding (and following activities) planned in his head.

---

[25] William Philo Clark was later promoted from an Army Lieutenant to Captain Clark.

Interrupting Sioux Bob's dream, Crazy Horse rode into Red Cloud Agency, Fort Robinson, Larrabee's trading post, and Nellie's life.

Never underestimate Crazy Horse.

> "...A man was thought to be more manly if he successfully seduced another's wife," (Sneve, p. 23).

Even if she wasn't married, no matter her suiters, Crazy Horse felt she was an eligible bride and courted her without the obvious rituals of dating.

Wasn't that what got him into trouble with No Water's wife?

Prudent to avoid the prenup rituals this time.

Step back over a month. Crazy Horse knew he had to surrender. He wasn't sure of the process or how to deal with upcoming activities at the fort.

Seeing wagon loads of rations arriving, Hang-Around-The-Fort Indians went out to meet Crazy Horse. Perhaps they thought they might get more rations or at least wanted early on to be on the good side of Crazy Horse. (Remember Red Cloud and Spotted Tail had concerns about all the attention given Crazy Horse.)

Even before his arrival in early May, Crazy Horse had been dealing with Lieutenant White Hat Clark. Around May third, Clark rode out to met Crazy Horse as his group progressed toward surrender. Clark required that all Crazy Horse followers lay down their guns and never to make war again.

Crazy Horse stepped forward, laid down his rifle at Lieutenant Clark's feet. All others followed. Guns piled up.

Back to Nellie....

Crazy Horse even talked to Clark about the eligibility of Nellie.

Speculation suggests that by June 1877 Captain Clark first winkingly approved the Nellie/Crazy Horse relationship. Keep in mind, the Army assigned Clark to be responsible for Crazy Horse.

As a longtime resident, Nellie would help keep Crazy Horse local. When Clark realized Nellie had eyes for Crazy Horse, Clark had second thoughts.

Not to waste time, Crazy Horse arranged to have some horses delivered to the Larrabee corral.

Obviously, Nellie, her father, and stepmother agreed to the arrangement. The horses stayed corralled.

Likely unknowingly the trader girl, Nellie with passionate interested in Crazy Horse, became a mechanism bridging the gulf between the U.S. Army, white society, Washington, and Red Cloud.

Summer solstice 1877 was quickly approaching symbolizing past and future.

As Crazy Horse's ragtag accumulation reached Fort Robinson, days were long and getting longer. Many things besides prairie flowers were budding in the spring of 1877.

Humans, like animal instincts, take advantage of long days, awakened before the sun, eat when food is available, utilize sunlight and rest based on length of night.

May 6, 1877, group sign-in at Fort Robinson and the subsequent eyeing of Nellie did not allow public relations with Crazy Horse. Forces were tugging at him as distrust abounded.

Chapter 16

Resettle

Crazy Horse was too independent to be confined to either the Red Cloud or Spotted Tail Agencies.

The Army knew that. Crazy Horse knew it.

Black Shawl was sick. Would she survive? What kind of second wife should he seek?

Was May 1877 the first time Crazy Horse met Nellie. Perhaps, but doubtful. Larrabee's trading post was too prominent and his daughters to obvious to ignore.

It's hard to figure out where Crazy Horse and his forces got ammunition and other simple supplies, like salt. Even if his contingent didn't get supplies directly from Long Joe, his followers likely had exchanged hides and pelts there.

Too many followers and too many trips had been made to the Spotted Tail and Red Cloud camps to not engage with the trading post which had been located in either Nebraska or South Dakota since at least since the spring of 1858 when son Philip Larrabee was born to Joseph and Mary Larrabee

It really doesn't matter when Crazy Horse first met Nellie. There were internal tribal and government political things to figure out. Nellie was a fascinating spousal choice.

Red Cloud, chief in charge, didn't trust Crazy Horse.

Indian scout and Crow/Sioux interpreter, Frank Benjamin Grouard (a.k.a. Standing Bear) sought to discredit Crazy Horse in his meetings with General George Crook.[56]

The year before on September 9, 1876, Crook lead a famished band of troops in northwest South Dakota. They came across a Sioux camp and raided it for food.

The following day, Crazy Horse and his followers, attacked Crook and his troops. Crazy Horse was defeated in what is known as the Battle of Slim Buttes.

General George Crook, who was the U.S. Army's Head of Department of the Platte when Crazy Horse surrendered wanted Crazy Horse to go to Washington to help finalize his own Indian Agency.

In an intriguing twist, on May 15, 1877 (a week after surrendering) General Crook, recruited Crazy Horse to be U.S. Indian Scout as a non-commissioned U.S.

Army officer. Crazy Horse was given military issued equipment including clothes and a pistol (Matson, p. 129).

Accounts differ on where Crazy Horse wanted his own reservation. Some claim he wanted the Black Hills. That is highly suspect for two very important reasons.

First, the Black Hills was booming with gold-crazy whites. By September 1877 when Crazy Horse surrendered, the Black Hills from south to north was a booming commerce center with law bordering on lawless.

For example, the northern Black Hills community in a valley full of dead trees, referred to as Dead Wood, had attracted hustlers, prostitutes, barkeeps, gamblers and gunslingers.

One such character, the infamous James Butler Hickok (1837-1876) better known as Wild Bill Hickok came to Deadwood, South Dakota to gamble in July 1876 with his lover, Martha Canary (1856-1903) best known as Calamity Jane.

To shorten the story, Crazy Horse avoided whites and did not trust them. Why would he want a reservation where game, especially buffalo, had been exterminated, and untrustworthy gold-crazed hoodlums were digging holes all of the Hills?

Within weeks of arriving in Deadwood, Wild Bill Hickok was playing poker in Nuttal & Mann's Saloon (better known now as Saloon #10).

The Black Hills and surrounding area was being developed. Buffalo were gone and cattle from Texas were arriving by the thousands. Hay was needed for the winter.

While gold was being searched, drunk miners caused all kinds of rowdiness. Meat was in demand. Hay was needed to feed them. On February 25, 1876, along the banks of Rapid Creek a square mile was plotted for the new town called Hay Camp--renamed Rapid City.[57]

Tuberculosis and other diseases were a problem.

Doctor James R. Walker gained national attention for treatment of tuberculosis while working on the Pine Ridge Reservation in the 1890s. Likely he treated Black Shawl.

Walker had other interests. Money.

With buffalo gone, beef was butchered for the Indians as Fire Thunder recalled in a 1930s interview.

> "Dr. Walker told some of us secretly he was pursuing a course whereby Texas Long-horns were to be brought up to graze on Oglala land, and we were all going to be rich because each month, each steer would bring in pay…."[58]

Spiritual peace of the Black Hills had been ruptured.

Poker games were going on night and day as players shifting tables in continuous play. Gunslinger

Hickok did not avoid gambling, but he avoided doing it with his back to a door—not August 2, 1876.

In a previous game, fellow-gambler, Jack McCall, known as Crooked Nose Jack, lost to Hickok. After consuming too much whisky, McCall slipped in the saloon's backdoor and immediately shot Hickok in the back of the head with a 45-caliber revolver.

Wild Bill Hickok, at the time, was holding a full-house (a pair of aces and three eights). Killed immediately, Hickok's blood flowed onto the table. Even today, as poker is played around the world a pair of aces and eights is known as a "Dead Man's Hand."

Crazy Horse took many chances over the years, so you could say he was also a gambler. But, in August of 1876 he was leading his camp protected by warriors through the border area of Montana and South Dakota trying to avoid U.S. Army repercussions of the Battle of Little Bighorn (June 25, 1876).

A month after a headshot killed Wild Bill Hickok, September 10, 1876, Crazy Horse was involved in the Battle of Slim Buttes (South Dakota) against the U.S. Army's third cavalry lead by Captain Anson Miles.

It was a year earlier, July 24, 1875, that white guys recorded the first climb to the top of Black Hill's highest peak at 7,244 feet then known as Harney Peak, renamed Black Elk Peak in 2016.

The accomplishment was by professor Henry Newton, a Captain Tuttle, Lieutenant Foote of the Jenny Newton Expedition fame, and Doctor Valentine T. McGillycuddy who was a Fort Robinson doctor that treated both Black Shawl for tuberculosis and Crazy Horse after he was stabbed.

Besides no buffalo around the Black Hills (infested with crazy whites), there was another reservation location desired by Crazy Horse. That was an area of known game. It was an area away from the Red Cloud and Spotted Tail Agencies.

Crazy Horse knew the area had good water, buffalo and grass in remote northwestern Wyoming. An area designated,

> "…by 1877 (General George) Crook became one of its strongest proponents. He believed agencies in the Yellowstone country had several benefits, including good bottom land for agriculture, a navigable river for supply, and one of the better remaining hunting ranges. More important the Indians would be far from the Black Hills miners and settlers."[59]

Lastly, Crazy Horse knew it was in the western most Lakota territory.

> "On the day his band surrendered, Crazy Horse said he wanted a new agency east of the White (Big Horn) Mountains or along Beaver

Creek in the Powder River country (of Wyoming)," (Buecker).

That location matched and area General Crook knew would separate Crazy Horse from his known opponents, Red Cloud and Spotted Tail, who were confined in a small area of northwest Nebraska long devoid of buffalo.

A strategist, like Crazy Horse, always has a backup plan. In his case, he would settle in beautiful water-fed area on Beaver Creek now called Teton, Wyoming (north of Jackson and south of the Yellowstone National Park).

That area still had pockets of buffalo and elk.

Though Crazy Horse would be physically separated from Red Cloud and Spotted Tail, they would have been extremely jealous. Crazy Horse's access to buffalo on a new reservation would have been a problem.

The other two Chiefs had Agency populations over 4,000 which were only getting limited beef rations. It would have been extremely likely far more than 899 initial followers would have joined Crazy Horse to his new Wyoming reservation.

If the only way Crazy Horse was to get a reservation was to go to Washington, Red Cloud and Spotted Tail had reasons to prevent him from going.

The day Crazy Horse surrendered,

> "Short Bull recalled that Crazy Horse plainly stated his priorities. Prepared to concede the Tongue River location, he insisted on is second-choice site: 'There is a creek over there they call Beaver Creek; there is a great flat west of the headwaters of Beaver Creek; I want my agency put right in the middle of that flat,'" (Bray, p. 297).

Crook wanted Crazy Horse to go to Washington to prove to higher-ups the "Indian Situation" as under control.

Crazy Horse declined Crook's May offer to go to Washington. Instead, he wanted to go on a Wyoming buffalo hunt. My hunch is he wanted to see how many buffalo still roamed in the Beaver Creek area south of Yellowstone.

Crook made another request in June 1877 when Crazy Horse acquiesced and again said he would go if he was given his own reservation in Wyoming.

Had Nellie been consulted?

What was her opinion?

Crazy Horse vacillated about going to Washington.

Would Nellie accompany Crazy Horse as a spouse, or interpreter, and be able to read Washington documents?

Someone or something changed the mind of Crazy Horse about going to Washington.

Confined to a railroad car for days, staying in a hotel, eating at a table, sitting on chairs I believe would have scared Crazy Horse more than meeting what whites called the great white father.

All the Army bigwigs had been at Fort Robinson. Nellie knew them. Also, Nellie had done all those other "white" things. Crazy Horse knew it and would have sought her help.

> "In June (1877) Crazy Horse made somewhat of a turnabout and declared that he would go to Washington after he was given an agency of his own in Wyoming," (Sajna, p. 309).

Was it Nellie?

> "…The courtship was conducted with some discretion," (Bray, p. 319).

We know he was privately meeting with Nellie. What did they discuss?

The Army had their favorite contractors—paid to freight supplies to meet Army and needs of the Indian Agencies. A fact that seems to be overlooked is that the Larrabee trading store was a competitive supplier of materials for Fort Robinson using the same suppliers, like bullwhacker Scotty Philip.

Though rations came from different contractors, Crazy Horse would have realized the connections he needed were at the Larrabee trading post.

Crazy Horse also realized it would not only be one trip to Washington. Upon return, within months, he would have had more invites.

Before Crazy Horse was born, eastern South Dakota's Chief Waneta had been to Washington several times and even to England.

Everyone at the Agency knew Red Cloud had been to Washington at least a couple times in the past decade. Crazy Horse would have realized that gave Red Cloud status amongst all at his Agency and beyond.

Building assurance of his well thought out plan, of how and where his followers would move, Crazy Horse,

> "Spent many hours planning for the day when he and his people could move there. He had even pinpointed a sacred place where we could keep our Sacred Calf Pipe. It was just south of what is now Rapid City, South Dakota," (Matson, p. 129).

Apparently, Crazy Horse had a secret hiding place where he would keep his ceremonial pipe. Until he settled in a place of his own, he likely contemplated a pipe-offering council with the pipe unused until then.

In July 1877 Crazy Horse began organizing a buffalo hunt into Wyoming. Perhaps he was scouting boundaries for his new agency or trying to determine if herds of buffalo still existed where he had hunted in the past.

More importantly, would the number of buffalo be sustainable for his followers? How many of the 899 would go with him? Would more want to follow him?

With beef rations a constant point of contention at the Red Cloud Agency, how many more followers would be dependent on the Wyoming buffalo herds?

Nellie would have known her father's trading post could not supply Crazy Horse and his crew necessities for his upcoming hunt, nor would it have been wise for Joseph Larrabee to offer guns and ammunition to him.

> "The stores of J.W. Dear and Frank Yates prepared to order new supplies…(of) powder, lead, and fixed ammunition (after) Lieutenant Clark received instructions from General Crook on (July) 28th…, (Bray, p. 322).

Nellie, fluent in Lakota and English, not only had close familiarity with Lieutenant Clark and Army operations, but she also had lived with the Red Cloud and Stopped Tail Indians for most of her life. Not to be overlooked was her family store.

It is very likely Nellie was not living with Crazy Horse yet in June 1878.

Chatter is useful when applied. No doubt Nellie informed her father of Crazy Horse's Wyoming hunt, potential new Wyoming agency, but also of supplies being ordered by the Dear and Yate's stores.

Who could Crazy Horse trust?

Not Red Cloud.

Spotted Tail had his doubts about Crazy Horse. No Water followers had their sites on him and intentions were not good.

One rumor was Crazy Horse would be killed in Washington for what he had done to Custer.

Tuberculosis was a serious—a death sentence for many. Crazy Horse had to think about what he would do if the love of his live, Black Shawl, had died.

Nellie offered hope.

Who knows? He might have lived a fruitful life with Nellie had he made the Washington trip.

Crazy Horse had to plan, and he could benefit from Nellie. Indications are they developed a trusting relationship.

Perception that Crazy Horse was quick to action before he thought out a plan is incorrect.

He won too many battles. He had to be a thoughtful planner.

After returning to camp, wherever it was, he would hang around others to hear what they had to say, then he would go off to contemplate.

I believe he cherished quiet time with Black Shawl, especially after they lost their two-year-old daughter, They Are Afraid of Her.

As Black Shawl grew less active with tuberculosis, Crazy Horse spend more time with her, but responsibility to his followers was too great to allow him to stay in camp day-after-day.

Once Crazy Horse arrived in Fort Robinson with his wife and 899 followers, his responsibilities did not diminish. First, he had to ensure government allocations were adequate. When he arrived, complaints abounded that rations were not sustainable at the Red Cloud Agency.

Secondly, Crazy Horse wanted his own Agency just like Red Cloud and Spotted Tail had their own agency. That was a constant conflict amongst the various competing factions. Would Crazy Horse draw more than his followers from existing Agencies?

Yes. Without a doubt.

How many?

That was Red Cloud's concern.

Other chiefs also had wanted agencies but didn't get them. Sitting Bull was still in Canada. He would be the last to turn himself in and it would have been very doubtful to expect a Sitting Bull reservation in the future.

If Crazy Horse didn't go to Washington, likely a new, and last reservation would have been allocated to someone else. For example,

> "Lone Horn proposed a third agency…(which included) all of our Black Hills…(as) discussed with government officials at the 1868 Fort Laramie treaty signing…. He did not feel up to the train ride to Washington, D.C.…(nor did he) understand the white man's language…" (Matson, p. 87).

Lone Horn trusted Black Tongue, who spoke some English and who's camp was close to the Spotted Tail Agency where Crazy Horse likely had his camp with wife, Black Shawl.

In the spring of 1874, Black Tongue made a trip by railroad to Washington to check the progress of Lone Horn's proposed agency. At the same time, U.S. Army General George Custer was in southeast Montana planning to move a thousand soldiers, a 110 wagons, and seventy Indian scouts to "explore" the Black Hills.

Custer's contingent came in from the north, through far northeast Wyoming. On July 18, 1874, Custer had his first glimpse of the Black Hills.

Crazy Horse, likely on a reconnaissance mission, saw Custer's group approaching and returned to report his sighting to his father, Worm, and others including Lone Horn.

Age, stress and regret for sending Black Tongue to Washington in his place was apparently too much for Lone Horn. He died in 1874 which passed on his responsibilities to his son, Touch The Cloud, who was Crazy Horse's friend that saved his life from No Water.

Touch The Cloud then made a trip to Washington, D.C. to see if the Black Hills had been reclaimed by the government in violation of the 1868 treaty. It had not.

However, by the spring of 1875 Touch The Cloud, Crazy Horse, Spotted Tail, Red Cloud and all subchiefs protested invasion of gold miners.

This background is critical to understand why, three years later, Nellie was needed to prepare Crazy Horse for his own trip to Washington, D.C.

He had friends, like Touch The Cloud, with Washington experience, but he also needed to understand what English speakers around him were saying and doing.

Nellie, with her father's contacts in trading, likely ability to read and write, knowledge of allocations and potential future allocations, and her ear out for rumors spouted by brag-a-dos soldiers, would all be needed to build his knowledge base for his own agency.

Crazy Horse, like Red Cloud, Spotted Tail, Lone Horn, and Touch The Cloud knew that a chief could not get his own agency and designated lands except if approved from Washington.

Pressure was immense. The Washington trip was scheduled. Should he go?

Chapter 17

Education and Rations

For a culture to survive, children had to carry on traditions. Settled in one spot, how would children be trained on the necessities of life?

What if Nellie could read?

Would she have been the first wife to accompany a Lakota chief to Washington?

Was she the first Lakota chief's wife to read and write?

Closing years of roaming and fighting by Crazy Horse was paralleled by development and spread of the written Lakota language.

It is certainly reasonable to believe Nellie could read and write English. However, I have no reason to believe Black Buffalo Woman, Black Shawl, or Nellie could read the newly written Dakota language.

It has been mentioned earlier that the Dakota language had been translated by missionary Stephan R. Riggs. The reverend Riggs and his wife, Mary, a trained teacher, were adamant about setting up schools to provide a formal education for Lakota youth and their eight children.[60]

(Ten years before Nellie was born) in 1843 near present day Saint Peter, Minnesota, Stephan Riggs opened a Dakota mission with Robert Hopkins at Traverse des Sioux. The Riggs continue to expand their missions and schools west.[61]

Some of their children pursued missionary work. In 1872 son, Thomas (1847-1940), accompanied his father to the Missouri River in central South Dakota and established "Hope Station." It served about three hundred Lakotans living across the River from Fort Sully.[62]

In 1874 Thomas Riggs transferred his school and mission to Peoria Bottom about five miles north of what is now the Oahe Dam which was completed on August 17, 1962. Riggs built a school, chapel, home, and livestock corrals which are now under about 150 feet of water.

The school/chapel (built in 1877 by as Sioux City, Iowa carpenter and local Indians) was salvaged, moved atop the Missouri River bluffs and still overlooks the Oahe Dam in 2026 next to a visitors' center.

An aerial view of the original Thomas Riggs development on Peoria Bottom is on display in the Oahe

Dam's Visitor's center next to the 149-year-old chapel. In that old photograph, next to the Riggs' place, is my in-laws, Art and Helen Metzinger's farm. That is where my wife, Patricia Metzinger, grew up and occasionally they were invited for special, formal meals at the Riggs'.

My point is that Lakota children were being taught English and Lakota reading and writing in the mid-1870s.

Riggs school was established too late for Nellie, as her family had moved to Montana likely in 1855. Having helped run the family trading post, the Larrabees likely had books, newspapers, and other reading materials for soldiers, white settlers, and Lakotans to browse.

The 2014 well footnoted version of John Neihardt's Black Elk Speaks points out specific fiction added by Neihardt, but also facts to supplement the book. Though Crazy Horse wasn't along,

> "A delegation of chiefs visited Washington in September 1877 and received President Hayes's promise that if they agreed to spend the winter on the Missouri, in the spring they could choose new agency sites within the Great Sioux Reservation," (Neihardt, p. 317).[63]

That was the same month Crazy Horse was killed (September 5, 1877).

Another point of contention by other authors was that Nellie acquired a ration or better an Indian allotment after Crazy Horse was killed.

Being half Cheyenne she was entitled to an allotment. Secondly, as a wife of Crazy Horse, she was entitled to rations and land allotment.

Even if Nellie had married a white man, like her older sister, Sarah, she would have been entitled to monthly rations. (More on Sarah will be explained a bit later on her contributions to Lakota's lifeblood, the buffalo.)

As Nebraska State Historical Society pointed out:

> "Products of unions between white fathers and Sioux women, the mixed-blood offspring of these marriages were often inelegantly referred to as "half-breeds" and their fathers as "squaw men" in the written records of the period. In the census the male parent does not normally appear as a tribal enrollee, nor were they beneficiaries of the ration and annuity system, but their wives and children were so entitled."[64]

Red Cloud was reliant on the Episcopal church to divvy food under President Grant's Indian Peace Plan. Schooling, and for that matter, missionary work, took far, far less priority that assigning and delivering food.

Scandals and scoundrels complicated assignment of rations while, incoming chiefs with different goals complicated Red Cloud's constantly reassembled group know at the time as the "Sod Agency" (later called the

Red Cloud Agency) then located north of the Platte River in Nebraska near the Wyoming border.

> "During the winter months, other Sioux bands from Yellowstone and Powder River country (Wyoming) filled the (Red Cloud) reservation, unhappy over eviction from hunting grounds...(and) imminent invasion of their last sanctuary to the north, *Paha Sapa*, the Black Hills, ...their chiefs quarreled as much among themselves as with the whites," (Keller, p. 118).[65]

The final arrival of Crazy Horse and his interests in his own agency in the summer of 1877 left his wife, Black Shawl, and second wife, Nellie, in a constant state of confusion.

Frustrating Red Cloud, Crazy Horse had negotiated to get an increase in rations.

> "Although Red Cloud's aims were confined to maintaining his own edge as principal Oglala chief...Crazy Horse had every reason to be satisfied...(with Lieutenant Clark). ...The following day brought more encouraging news. At the regular ration issue, Black Shawl and other claimants were issued new tickets...(after) revised census, Dr. Irwin had authorized ration increases of fifteen percent...(including) beef ration." (Bray, p. 322).

Lakota had been living on a high protein diet for a century. With thousands of people living on or around the Red Cloud encampment, beef was in very high demand. As a replacement for the buffalo, beef was the primary protein ration item.

Texas cattle, were driven north, grazed and filled U.S. Army and Episcopal church demand for meat.

Crazy Horse's future brother-in-law created an unexpected development.

Chapter 18

Allow multiple wives?

Black Buffalo Woman

Mistress of Crazy Horse, Black Buffalo Woman, was a stain on his reputation.

Many authors have suggested that Crazy Horse had married his mistress. Be cautious of Internet searches. The on-line Free Encyclopedia, Wikipedia, states, "Black Shawl….was Crazy Horse's second wife."[66]

Those references implied Black Buffalo Woman would have been his first wife.

I agree with most historians who recognized Lakota customs. Black Buffalo Woman was a mistress.

Evidence:

1. The Lakota council required Crazy Horse give up his coveted title as Shirt Wearer.

2. No Water paid Crazy Horse for shooting him but did not pay Crazy Horse to get his wife, Black Buffalo Woman, back.
3. Black Elk, cousin to Crazy Horse, in his book **Black Elk Speaks**, makes only a one sentence mention of being shot by No Water without giving details. Why?

In the many hours John Neihardt interviewed Black Elk, to my knowledge he never detailed Black Buffalo Woman's relationship with Crazy Horse

It is common practice, even reverent, not to mention indiscretions of the deceased.

Black Elk, a candidate for sainthood by the Roman Catholic Church, was a well-spoken Lakota elder. He had a polite way and avoided degrading even those he disliked.

Regarding the Crazy Horse affair with Black Buffalo Woman, Black Elk quoted only one sentence and it referenced only two Crazy Horse wounds.

> "He was fifteen years old when he was wounded by accident; and the other time was when he was a young man and another man was jealous of him because the man's wife liked Crazy Horse," (Neihardt, p. 53.)

What a gift of understatement.

Black Shawl

Black Shawl was Crazy Horse's first wife. He loved her and had a child together that unfortunately died.

Confirmed: Black Shawl was a wife.

Nellie Larrabee

Moving to a third issue, was Crazy Horse allowed to take Nellie as a second wife?

The Morrill Anti-Bigamy Act signed by President Abraham Lincoln July 8, 1862, prohibited multiple spouses. That was a Congressional Act signed by the President eleven years before Crazy Horse married Nellie.

Did the U.S. then recognize Nellie as being married to Crazy Horse?

Yes.

Why?

There were likely four reasons.

1. The Morrill Anti-Bigamy Act of 1862 was implemented against the Mormon movement after their church founder, Brigham Young, declared on August 28, 1852, that bigamy was a legitimate church sanctioned union.

2. Multiple wives were common amongst Lakota.
3. The U.S. Constitution's 14th Amendment adopted in 1868 did not consider Native Americans citizens, even though they were born in what was then the United States.
4. Nellie, being half Cheyenne, and her sisters were given rations and land allotment since they were considered Indians.

Nellie lived with Crazy Horse and Black Shawl from the summer of 1877 until his death. She was Crazy Horse's second wife, and he had a right to marry her.

To briefly dispense of any notion otherwise, keep in mind the U.S. did not tax Indians because they were "alien nations" living within United States boundaries.

The U.S. Supreme Court in an 1884 decision on Elk v. Wilkins ruled that Elk, though born in Nebraska on a reservation, was not a U.S. citizen. Therefore, Elk did not have a right to vote.

It is similar to current disagreements about illegal immigrant or tourist's children having an automatic right to be U.S. citizens because they were born in the United States. Indians, like Elk, did not. That changed with the 1924 Indian Citizenship Act.

Perhaps based on Supreme Court action, similar national legislation needs to be passed to allow or deny automatic U.S. birthright citizenship.

Reservation Indians, though born in the United States did not receive birthright citizenship until 1924.

Crazy Horse had three stepmothers all at the same time after his father, Worm, married three sisters. They were all living when Crazy Horse was killed. Lakota culture therefore allowed Worm and thereafter his son, Crazy Horse, to marry Nellie.

Now for the 1862 Morrill Anti-Bigamy Act: Because Crazy Horse was an Indian on one of many "alien nation" reservations, that precluded him from complying with the Anti-Bigamy Act.

The forth issue, Nellie and her sisters getting Indian rations and allotments, will be considered when discussing Crazy Horse's white brothers-in-law.

Chapter 19

Tasks

There is no way to underestimate the tasks, duties, and responsibilities of Indian women. As men were responsible for providing meat, protecting families, and deciding council policy, women took care of camps, and matured to offer advice.

As an outside observer explaining activities a century and a half earlier, it seems women accepted their jobs without questioning workload.

Ella Deloria and other accounts explain duties of Lakota women, (Albers, p. 238).

At camp, women:

- erected tipi,
- prepared bedding,
- gathered firewood,
- selected tipi and pony drag poles,
- tended fire,

- hauled water,
- managed food supplies,
- cooked,
- served food,
- served men's counsel,
- made cooking utensils,
- cleaned pelts and hides,
- processed meats for storage,
- made tipi,
- decorated tipi,
- kept tipi organized,
- made clothes,
- were midwives,
- cared for children,
- babysat for others,
- picked berries,
- collected spices and medical herbs,
- through experience offered advice, and
- other domestic duties.

Lakota were a roaming people. Women didn't decide to move, that was up to the men. Travel, whether for catching up with roaming buffalo, finding better protection or water resources, avoid or prepare enemy attacks, and travel for other reasons the women relied on men until it was moving day.

When moving, women:

- organized camp to move,
- packed everything,
- organized food for travel,
- carried children or cared for them on pony drags,
- organized and managed travel supplies,
- set up temporary or semipermanent camps,
- erected tipi, which was followed by
- all women's duties at camp.

Some white women when they first married into an Indian family camp, wanted only one husband. However, after considering all the assigned duties of a women, another wife or two was considered beneficial.

It was common to have a wife's sister or sisters as second or third wives. Some chiefs, like Sitting Bull, had multiple wives not all related. Some were war captives.

As Virginia Driving Hawk-Sneve explained, original white descriptions of women's work was written from European white privilege. European women of status had attendants who did the manual labor. Indian women shared their work, not assigned it.

> "...Indian women's work was essential to the tribes well being and survival just as much as the man's hunting which provided meat, and his

skills as a warrior which protected the women, children and elders," (Driving Hawk-Sneve, p. 3).

Neither women nor men should be presented as overworked or privileged. To grasp demographics, it is important to understand the ratio of male warriors hunters compared to those who remained at camp.

Although roaming groups of Lakota likely made counts of lodges, and how many warriors they could assemble when necessary, they did not publish a census.

Perhaps the best way to get a handle on the ratio of men, women and children is to look at the May 6, 1877, census of 899 people that surrendered with Crazy Horse.

There were:

- men –217 (24.1%)
- women—312 (34.7%)
- male children—186 (20.7%) and
- female children—184 (20.5%).

Women vs. men seems to be the most obvious demographic irregularity. Differences are more startling than reported.

The world's sex ratio is 105 baby boys born to 100 girls.[67] Interestingly, that is about the ratio of male children to female children reported in Crazy Horse's surrender group.

The real question may be, how many warriors were available to protect the Crazy Horse contingent?

First, let's assume the U.S. Army census of those arriving with Crazy Horse in category "children" were likely under the age of fifteen.

Given the ratio of children under fifteen, one would expect that 62 boys and 61 girls were still under twenty.

Also, the number of senior men, including those with immobility to fight, may be similar to the ratio of men to women. That would mean approximately 135 were over age sixty accounting for about 55 men and 80 women.

When warriors left for battle, no doubt some men remained at camp due to previous injuries. For example, Sitting Bull was courageous but walked with a limp from apparent hip and ankle injuries.

Injured men and seniors would have protected camps supported by young teenagers while warrior/hunters were gone.

It is reasonable to assume that when Crazy Horse surrendered, he would have had only about 150 battle-ready warriors at his disposal. That number would have included about sixty-two teenagers (boys fifteen to age twenty).

Consequently, of the 217 men that surrendered May 6, 1877, at Fort Robinson, only about a hundred or so would have been experienced to stage a raid on Army troops like the June 25-26, 1876, when Custer was killed at the Battle of Little Bighorn.

This background is provided to understand that Lakota women worked hard and had plenty of tasks. Fit men able to fight were few by comparison.

Women at camp, including girls fifteen and older, would have had to feed and care for all the children, elderly, injured and sick.

Chapter 20

Adjustments

There were other outside activities that influenced agency social life and even meals.

Red Cloud and Spotted Tail Agencies were located near Fort Robinson in Nebraska. Nebraska turned from a U.S. Territory to become a state in 1867—ten years before Crazy Horse surrendered and was killed.

While churches, missionaries, and church-schools were being developed in and around reservations and Agencies, colleges were being established.

The Morrill Act, known as the Land Grant College Act of 1862, promoted agricultural and mechanical teaching and research. Each state was allocated a minimum of 30,000 acres of federal government land to establish at least one state college.

Two years after statehood, Nebraska's legislature established the University of Nebraska-Lincoln in 1869 and was awarded an additional 130,000 acres of federal land to be used for agricultural purposes.

There were three functions of Morrill's Land Grant Act: teaching, research and spreading the new knowledge.

Agricultural research in far northwest Nebraska was not fully functional until 1909. That is when the Panhandle Research and Extension Station under the University of Nebraska-Scottsbluff was opened.[26]

Red Cloud and Spotted Tail Agencies benefitted indirectly from passage of the Morrill Act.

For example, once Crazy Horse's group of 899 was all registered on May 7, 1877, food was allocated.

Women that arrived with Crazy Horse had no experience using the new food raw materials like flour, yeast, sugar, and lard.

Nellie had experience with not only those foods, but also beef which had the same components as buffalo but different proportional cuts and uses.

---

[26] The University of Nebraska-Scottsbluff has the only publicly funded proso millet varietal breeding station in the U.S. Unfortunately, that millet research was not developed until the Red Cloud and Spotted Tail Agencies were moved to southern South Dakota.

Black Shawl's respiratory illness had manifested throughout her painful body causing her arm to swell. Preparing and cooking food would have been difficult.

On the day of Crazy Horse's group enrollment at Fort Robinson, May 7th, rations were allocated to the new arrivals. Many did not know how to use the new food supplies.

> "(Women) gathered on the campground to be taught the use of some of the new comestibles.[27] Supplied with skillets and flour, they observed (General Geroge) Crook's ubiquitous packer, Tom Moore,[28] demonstrate the preparations of fry bread—already a major item in the agency Lakota diet," (Bray, p. 297).

By 1877, it is doubtful that Thomas Moore had been trained to demonstrate cooking techniques supported by the University of Nebraska.

As Morrill's Land Grant colleges were being developed starting in the 1860s, the logical result of college teaching and research was to pass new knowledge to statewide audiences. Local farm groups, women's clubs and other such organizations sought speakers who were

---

[27] Comestibles are edible foods or components that can be made into meals.

[28] Thomas Moore led mule packs and obviously knew how to cook in the open with any native and available supplies during General Crook's travels from 1866 to 1878.

familiar with agricultural, mechanical, and domestic research.

Parts of Indian allocated lands was suitable for farming while much of it was only good for grazing cattle.

When cattle was supplied to Agencies and later Reservations, they were eaten. When seeds, like wheat and corn, was supplied for planting, it was ground, cooked and eaten.

Roaming tribes like the Lakota had not farmed nor domesticated animals, except horses which were hobbled with a rock wrapped in a leather strap hung about the horse's neck.

Rocks found on prairie plains with a distinct worn band around the center were thought to be Indian hammers. Most were horse hobbles.[68]

In the 1960s when checking his cattle, my father-in-law, Arthur Metzinger, found a smooth glaciated rock in his pasture south of Blunt, South Dakota. It had a distinct manmade carved ring around the center.

(Photo of Indian hammer or horse hobble found by Arthur Metzinger in his grass pasture south of Blunt, South Dakota.)

One day while in Blunt shopping he met Luther Big Eagle on the sidewalk. Arthur mentioned finding an

Indian hammer on his land. Mr. Big Eagle laughed and said,

> "Everyone thinks they found an Indian hammer. What you found was a horse hobble. That is why you find them scattered throughout grassland rather just in areas, like around creeks, suitable for campsites."

Obviously, Indian women used all available tools for preparing and cooking foods. Smooth flat rocks were used as cutting boards or a platform for grinding seeds, berries, and meat. Another smooth rock was used to pound and tenderize tough wild game meat.

In the summer of 2025, I picked several gallons of wild chokecherries from the Black Hills. Nine gallons of juice was extracted. Though freezing most, I made a chokecherry crisp as a desert and gave some to my elderly Lakota friend, Victor Swallow.

Victor readily welcomed my treat and went on to tell me about how his mother, her mother, and his great grandmother used to also pick wild chokecherries on the Pine Ridge Reservation. (Victor called them cherries.)

To my surprise, Victor said Lakota women did not extract the hard pit. Instead, the chokecherry, skin, pulp and pit were pounded between two rocks into a thick paste. (Juice was saved as it ran from the rocks.)

Buffaloberries, like chokecherries, were also picked and pounded to make a nutritious food called pemmican when mixed with buffalo or other wild game meats.

Dried and preserved, pemmican, was easy for warriors and hunters to pack, haul, and eat while away from home camp.

Obviously, women were in charge of picking all plums and berries, drying all meat, and making all pemmican.

One day I was at Victor's house and I noticed a string of dried tannish roots, each about two to three inches long and about an inch wide, tied together and hanging on the doorway into his kitchen.

I asked, "What are those roots?"

Eighty-six-year-old Victor, who had lost his wife during the Covid 19 pandemic, smiled and said I picked those wild turnips and I'm making some soup with them tonight.

Several years ago my wife, daughter, and I visited Indian Grinding Rock Historic State Park in the Sierra Nevada foothills several miles from Jackson, California (east of Sacramento). The park is 135 acres with 1,185 mortar holes several inches deep.

Those holes had been used for centuries by resident Indians to pound acorns to powder. Collected a few days each fall, acorns made into powder would have been used in cooking for a full year.

Similar holes, but smaller, have been found in rocks in northwest Minnesota and far northeast part of South Dakota not far from the Kensington Stone now housed in a museum in Alexanderia, Minnesota

Theories of those hole origins include fourteenth-century Viking travers made holes for mooring their boats. Other's have suggested those holes were used to support sticks or rods which marked Viking property lines since similar property markings have been found in Norway.

It is not unlikely that Native Indians for centuries used and reused holes in Minnesota and South Dakota rocks as a mortar similar to the rock holes found in California. When grinding grain, seeds, or pits to edible powder, rocks and hardwoods were used as pestles.

These are just a few of the many ways Native women used plants and rocks as tools to prepare and preserve foods.

Arriving in Fort Robinson, handed cast-iron pots and pans, bags of flour and packages of yeast, Black Shawl would have been as perplexed on how to use them as were other incoming Indian women—except Nellie.

It wasn't until the Dawes Act of 1887 that Lakota men and women were routinely given farming equipment and allocated 160 acre plots of land.

Also, the Smith-Lever Act, signed into law in 1914, created the Cooperative Extension Services to be the third arm (or result) of the 1862 Land Grant Act. Before then it would have been up to Army cooks, traveling packers, like Thomas Moore, or experienced cooks, like Nellie, to train Black Shawl and others how to use white man's foodstuffs.

Lakota elder, Victor Swallow, wrote down an oral story about his maternal great grandmother, Bird All Over, who was born in in the 1850s.

> "… Bird All Over said when they were issuing rations they got sacks of flour among the rations and didn't know what it was used for. So they dumped out the flour and made dresses out of the sacks."

Cloth was issued. Not clothes. Without access to new hides, women would have to utilize any new cloth materials.

Victor continued:

> "Some Lakota lady who married a white man asked for the flour and everybody gave her the flour. Not once did they bother to ask her what she did with the flour. Later someone finally asked what the lady used the flour for and she taught them how to make bread with it," (Swallow, p. 46).

Thanks to Lakota women and men, like Victor, who wrote down oral stories. Those stories allowed us to understand the transition from living in the wild off nature to being restricted to one camp and issued unfamiliar foodstuffs.

Two hundred years ago Lakota women were using Stone Age technology—no frying pans, metal utensils, or the ubiquitous cast iron Dutch oven only invented in 1710.

Compared to roaming tribes using open fire cooking, buried in coals the covered metal Dutch oven cooked foods as did Arikara and settled tribes using pottery.

Herbs and stems tucked on the side of flames produced flavored meats completely different than fresh and died herbs mixed in covered pots.

Settled in agencies, the Northern Cheyenne, Lakota and Arapaho women began to switch cooking methods to match whites and settled tribes.

How did the women learn to change?

Passed from great grandmother, to grandmother, to mother to son, Victor Swallow wrote:

> "There are many stories told to me about acts of sharing," (Swallow, p. 8).

Growing a crop is one thing, preserving and using it was another unknown.

For example, once Lakota were settled on reservations men were taught agricultural techniques which had always been women's work.

Men: How to grow corn?

Women: How to preserve it?

One sharing story happened about a hundred years ago because a Mexican worker stopped by.

> "Mother talked about a Mexican whose first name was José. He taught them how to take care of corn.
>
> "My oldest uncle Stern Two Bulls, who was born 18 days after Wounded Knee (December 29, 1891), started digging a well close to his house. It was about 8 feet wide and more than 5 feet deep.
>
>> "José built a big fire that had a deep bed of coals in the hole. Then they brought several wagon loads of white corn, husks and all, and dumped them on top of the coals. Then they poured several buckets of water, put tarps over, then shoveled dirt on top trapping all the heat and water.
>>
>> "The next morning they got the dirt and tarps off and had lots of steamed corn which they braided some, cut others,

> and put them on drying racks," (Swallow, pp. 8-9).

There must be many such stories. Unfortunately, many are not written for our learning.

Research indicates Black Shawl, familiar with Lakota tradition of multiple wives, welcomed the use of unknown foods, medicine, sewing, and cooking assistance of Nellie.

Chapter21

Rumors

Black Shawl was sick.

May 7, 1877, the day after arriving, Crazy Horse requested the Army's attending doctor, Valentine T. McGillycuddy, to go his tipi to examine Black Shawl (Bray, p. 297). Apparently, she was weakened by the strenuous trip and suffering from tuberculosis.

Bray also claimed Crazy Horse had been secretly meeting and dating Nellie since June. Supposedly, August 2nd Nellie made a woman-to-woman call on Black Shawl.

Before Crazy Horse returned to his tipi, Black Shawl agreed to Nellie becoming wife number two. While neighboring women's gossip spread, Nellie stepped from the tipi and announced Black Shawl's acceptance. Crazy Horse consented by requesting Nellie to get her things and move in.

Planning for a buffalo hunt was well underway. Crazy Horse was to lead the hunters from early August into September. While away hunting for several weeks, he could rest easier knowing Nellie could care for Black Shawl.

Leadership at Spotted Tail and Red Cloud Agencies spread rumors that Crazy Horse's hunting trip was secretly a guise to head north with weapons and ammunition to join Sitting Bull who was already in Canada.

Since Crazy Horse surrendered, he drew attention, gifts, and special recognition.

> "Red Feather, the younger brother of Crazy Horse's first wife (Black Shawl) and a member of his band said, 'All the white people come to see Crazy Horse and gave him presents and money. The other Indians at the agency got very jealous,'"(Markley & Cutsforth, p. 103.)[69]

With the hunt delayed, more likely cancelled, Lieutenant Clark continued to press Crazy Horse to confirm he would go to Washington in mid-September.

One version has Nellie advising Crazy Horse that the hunting delay was a government ruse to distract him. Eventually, he would be attacked and imprisoned. Possibly, once he was on the way to Washington (scheduled for mid-September) he, like others, would be sent to Oklahoma or Florida.[70]

Crazy Horse had plenty of enemies within both the Red Cloud and Spotted Tail camps. Rumors intensified about his escape north pretending to hunt which led Lieutenant Clark and his superiors to question Crazy Horse's hunting intentions.

Intrigue heightened. Crazy Horse rumors spread through the Agencies, Camp Robinson, Camp Sheridan, and even newspapers.

Nellie had free reign on Fort Robinson, at her father's store[29] and the Agencies. She could obviously pick up rumors and bring them back to Crazy Horse.

> "Long Joe Larribee…supplied both the soldiers and the Sioux with goods they wanted. His cabin stood between the fort (Robinson) and the (Red Cloud) Agency…" (Veglahn, p. 45).[71]

Nellie had secreted her love for Crazy Horse and was right to question why Red Cloud and Spotted Tail Agency councils agreed with the Army to ensure Crazy Horse would go to Washington.

Rumors.

Gossip.

---

[29] Joe Larrabee, the long-time trader, was called a "civilian worker" at Camp Robinson according to the Clown family (Matson, p.131). He likely was an intermediary between the Army and Indians speaking different languages.

Rumors.

Here are a few:

One rumor was that Crazy Horse would be killed in Washington to get revenge on him for killing Custer only a short year before.

A contrary version was that Nellie, a mere teenager, was sent to spy on Crazy Horse and report back to Lieutenant Clark.

For those seeking intrigue, another version was that Nellie, being only sixteen years old, was taken to Crazy Horse tipi by her father. The intent was that young Nellie would stay in Crazy Horse's tipi to care for the sickly Black Shawl. In this version, Nellie was never Crazy Horse's wife.

Instead, as a teenager, in this version Nellie was trying to impress Fort Robinson soldiers with her knowledge of Crazy Horse.

Why stop there?

True or not, it is easy to compound rumors.

Those wanting a quick reference to Nellie and Crazy Horse will likely use free media Wikipedia which claims Nellie was sent by the Army to spy on Crazy Horse.[72]

Another version is that Red Cloud arranged to have Nellie, "a young woman" to live with Crazy Horse.[73]

To juice up the story, a U.S. Army scout William "Billie" Garnett (a.k.a. Billy Hunter) occasionally acted as an interpreter who also spied on Red Cloud, Cheyenne's Chief Dull Knief, and others. Perhaps jilted Garnett, who had children from at least three divorced wives, suggests Crazy Horse was caught in a sex trap. He claimed Nellie was "...a half-blood, not of the best frontier variety, an indivious and evil woman."[74]

The Edward Clown family claimed,

> "Nellie had a good heart and told Iron Cedar she would help her take care of Black Shawl," (Matson, p. 130).

Where did the Clown family get their information published in 2016?

> "Our knowledge of our family tree was given to us by our family elders," (Matson, p. 16). "We are happy that we finally have gotten our oral history into print," (Matson, p. 202).

It has been nearly 150 years since Crazy Horse was killed. Many, many stories have circulated about him. Obviously, historical fiction has crept into many.

Crazy Horse did not write a biography, nor did his wives.

What is true?

This book is an attempt to really understand Crazy Horse and the women that were in his life.

As stated above, some versions try to emphasize that Nellie was a teenager. In one reference she was fourteen[75]

In another version, Nellie was sixteen when introduced to Crazy Horse (Matson, p. 131). Many references I've read she was a teenager.

Why did Crazy Horse seek out Nellie?

Crazy Horse knew Nellie could speak multiple languages including English, Lakota, and most likely her mother and step-mother's language, Cheyenne. After developing a trusting relationship, he relied on Nellie as a source of camp gossip and news at Camp Robinson.[76]

Gossip continued.

Not to be outdone, each commentator tends to twist the relationship to attract attention to their version of the life of Crazy Horse.

Another storyline was that Nellie moved out of the Larrabee home suddenly. A couple days later, Joseph Larrabee found her in Crazy Horse tipi and was frustrated that she left without telling her stepmother, and many sisters and brothers.

In another version Joe Larrabee, Nellie's father, brought his young daughter and offered her to Crazy Horse.

Oral stories, especially rumors, have a way of manifesting into untruths or half-truths based on the need to vilify to justify continued babble.

A person writing about Nellie's family stated,

> "Larabee had a large family, including some good looking grown daughters. The oldest daughter, Helen, was in Crazy Horse's camp now, the wife of the Oglala chief," (Lee, p.54).

Nellie was not the oldest. In fact, she had an older married sister, Sarah, who had young boy.

Supporting evidence confirms Joseph Larrabee supplied Indians at Red Cloud camp when it was established in the 1860s. He also supplied the Red Cloud Agency which was renamed Pine Ridge Reservation and lived amongst the Lakota until his death in 1890.

Thereafter, most of the Larrabee children, like Nellie, lived with Lakota their entire lives.

Smears of one's character amongst a Lakota community was perpetuated not by people living amongst the Larrabees but authors trying to juice up their stories.

Perhaps Nellie only supported Black Shawl for a couple months (July and August 1877) while Crazy Horse contemplated the Army request to go to Washington, D.C.

There is support for the idea that Crazy Horse took his wife, Black Shawl, to the Spotted Tail Agency so she could be cared for by her relatives.

Then Crazy Horse was escorted back to Fort Robinson.[30] Nellie apparently stayed at Fort Robinson while Crazy Horse took the sick Black Shawl to the Spotted Tail Agency, (Matson, pp. 136-138).

Care for his wife, Black Shawl, took precedence.

Crazy Horse wanted to insure Black Shawl was in the best hands while he was gone on the postponed hunting trip, check the layout of his potential agency, or to prepare a couple weeks for the upcoming trip to Washington which he was being heavily recruited to take.

Death by smallpox, cholera, influenza, and tuberculosis was a constant reminder to prepare for the inevitable loss of Black Shawl.

Would she survive?

How long?

Would she need constant care?

Only four short years earlier, Crazy Horse and Black Shawl's only daughter, They Are Afraid of Her, a

---

[30] The name Fort Robinson is used in this book and by many authors to minimize reader's confusion. Actually the temporary "Tent Robinson" was named "Camp Robinson" March 29, 1874. It was not named "Fort Robinson" until December 1878, over a year after Crazy Horse was killed there.

tender little one of two or three, the love of their lives, died like many others of the water-borne disease cholera.

Would Black Shawl provide the homefront needed for Crazy Horse during these trying times?

No doubt those questions were discussed by Black Shawl and Crazy Horse before Nellie was accepted as a wife.

Black Shawl's move to the Spotted Tail Agency, forty (plus) miles away, also would have allowed Nellie and Crazy Horse to focus on impending decisions including the best way to get his own agency.

Nellie used her connections at Fort Robinson and the Red Cloud Agency (where she was living) to keep Crazy Horse up to date on ever-changing plans.

Crazy Horse had blended into the large Larrabee family.

> "Joseph Larabee and his wife vividly recalled their shock at the death of Crazy Horse, probably because he was their son-in-law," (Lee, p. 89).

One must seriously question many of the versions, often repeated by others. They assume Crazy Horse was easily dupped by Army's General George Crook, Fort Robinson commander, Lieutenant Colonel Luther Bradley, Agent Lee, Red Cloud, Spotted Tail, Nellie's father and others.

For example, Lieutenant W.P. Clark is credited with arranging the match early in 1877.

> "Joe Laribee's fourth daughter, Helen, had only lived in the lodge of Crazy Horse between May and the date of the great Oglala's death September 5, 1877," (Robinson, p. 76).

Crazy Horse had every right to be suspicious especially of anyone representing the Army, Red Cloud, Spotted Tail, supporters of No Water, and many others.

To suggest Crazy Horse was easily lured by a teenage girl borders on preposterous.

Besides, one only has to check Larrabee family history and cemetery records to see that Nellie (depending on her unknown day of birth) was twenty-three or twenty-four years old in 1877. The age of her older and younger siblings confined her birth to 1853.

Facts are hard to determine when various entities have reasons to spin narratives.

Rumors are usually devised and spread by those wanting to ignore the truth.

Truths are innate.

As Horace wrote over two thousand years ago, "Nothing is swifter than rumor."[31]

---

[31] Horace is the modernized name for ancient Roman poet, Quintus Horatius Flaccus (65-8 B.C.).

Crazy Horse listened in councils. Seldom spoke.

As his wise cousin Black Elk, explained, Crazy Horse often contemplated in his own tipi.

Confined and quiet he listened to his wives--Black Shawl as sedentary and Nellie the forward one.

Those were troubled times for Crazy Horse. He was caught between angry Lakota divisions, Army requirements, and frustratingly low rations for his people.

His wives' loving council and quiet uplifting voices would have soothed his soul.

Constantly considering how to free his people, Crazy Horse used leverage to get his own reservation before he consented to go to Washington.

Had he settled down and been able to read, Crazy Horse would have likely been enthralled with the ancient Roman writings of Horace who rhetorically proclaimed, "Who then is free? The wise man who can govern himself."

Chapter 22

Cultural Surrender

Restoration of the buffalo was the dream of Crazy Horse. His goal was to have his own reservation where buffalo could roam to carry on Lakota's traditional way of life.

The water-fed area of western Wyoming fit his needs. The Plains had changed. Buffalo were gone.

Culturally, Lakota men were in charge of everything outside the camp. Scouting, protection, hunting and making flint arrowheads occupied the men for centuries. Boys were likely tasked with finding flint.

(Photo of broken flint arrowhead found by Walter Wietgrefe Jr. on his wind-blown field in northcentral South Dakota during the 1930s.)

Cultures clashed. One used technology developed for their area; the other used technology brought into the Plains.

Once Lakota captured horses, how did they restrain them without fences?

They invented a horse grazing system by attaching a stone on a leather strap tied around the horses neck. Whites needed large areas fenced for grazing making horse capture difficult.

Plains Indians dressed in leather and wore moccasins. The U.S. Army arrived in blue uniforms with shiny buttons and brass. Before battle, which was easier to spot? Which could be heard arriving?

Blacksmiths were a must in Army camps. One major job was to make horseshoes. Plains Indians hooves were worn to keep trimmed or flint knives were used to trim hooves—likely more in winter.

Flint was chipped to form arrowheads. Wood was smoothed to form arrow shafts. Feathers were added to arrow shafts to stabilize flight and improve accuracy. On the other hand, extra powder was added to guns to blow out musket balls. Arrow dynamics (now called aerodynamics) was used to improve bullet flight.

Who learned from whom?

Women were in charge of camps. Food, lodging and all preparations were women's work.

What were Lakota men to do confined to Agencies and eventually Reservations?

Should women run all domestic affairs of the camp like in the past?

A major cultural shift was taking place.

Less than two hundred years earlier, Sioux moved from the Great Lakes area to the eastern Plains. A hundred years before Crazy Horse surrendered, Lakota broke off to claim the western plains occupied by the generally friendly Northern Cheyenne.

The Crow, after getting horses in the 1730s dominated the western Plains from South Dakota into Wyoming and Montana. That area, soon to be controlled by the Lakota, also had horses by then.

Horses allowed more mobility for men hunting and for women to move camps.

Since pony drags could more than quadruple the carry of dogs, women also could have more room in their family tipi.

Since living around the western Great Lakes, the Sioux had not been confined. Then men could hunt. In Agencies and on Reservations men could no longer hunt. Game were gone or scarce. Without hunting, Lakota did not need guns—the Army saw to that.

Lakota society was changing faster than women could have babies.

The Plains hosted the last Indians living in the wild. Crazy Horse, Sitting Bull and others eventually submitted to change.

Two hundred years ago Lakota had no wheel. Wheelless dog drags were their beast of burden and transport until the Sioux acquired horses from the Arikara.

Human legs were their only means of transportation before the horse.

Compare Sioux to the history of others. Has there been any culture that transitioned from Stone Age so quickly?

In 2026 Victor Swallow is eighty six. His Lakota great grandparents transitioned from the wild to electricity within decades. No wonder their decedents had difficulty adjusting.

Domesticated camels were given to the Biblical character, Abraham, by an Egyptian Pharaoh 4,000 years ago. Camels could haul more and farther when Abraham already had donkeys which were domesticated in Africa a thousand years before he lived.

No American buffalo were domesticated before the death of Crazy Horse. Yet, cattle were domesticated in the Near East about 10,500 years ago.

With abundant game, especially millions of buffalo, there was no reason for the 25,000 Lakota to domesticate buffalo.

The Sioux inherited domesticated dogs from earlier Natives. Wolves and coyotes interbred with Lakota dogs which made them more aggressive and stronger.

Seed selection, farming, permanent living structures, and the wheel came of use in the Neolithic or "New Stone Age" period about 12,000 years ago.

Lakota made no mechanical inventions, although they were unique tipi dwellers. They made novel uses of all components of the buffalo.

Copper and bronze were refined 5,000 years ago. No raw metal resources were refined by Lakota.

Stones were shaped and used as tools and arrowheads into the last 1800s. Metal arrowheads were only introduced when guns were more lethal hunting or protection weapons.

Two hundred years ago Sioux had no written language.

Sumerians of Mesopotamia developed a written language about 5,000 years ago.

Two thousand years ago Jesus told a parable about ten virgins waiting for the bridegroom. Half had oil in their lamps, other foolish ones did not have enough oil to last the night.[32]

When Crazy Horse surrendered, Lakota did not have lamps, nor crushed or refined oil to put in them. I've never read that they extracted honey and used beeswax with a wick for making or lighting candles.

Fences. Lakota had no need for fences. Buffalo ran wild.

When Crazy Horse surrendered, buffalo had been hunted to near extinction in his area.

Sitting Bull did the same in the area of Canada where they settled. It wasn't their fault. Buffalo were thought to be unlimited until they were nearly gone.

Expansion of railroads into Lakota country wasn't the only cause of decimation.

After hearing that some buffalo remained, the Smithsonian Museum's chief taxidermist, William Hornaday, was sent to Montana arriving May 9, 1886, to collect eighty to a hundred buffalo for the Museum before they went extinct. By then buffalo sightings were very rare.

Hornaday's expert hunters only killed a couple on the spring trip so he returned in September. They hunted buffalo until December and killed only twenty-three. The

---

[32] Holy Bible, Matthew 25:1-13.

following year, Daniel Giraud Elliot, Smithsonian naturalist searched for three months and found no live buffalo—only bones (Hedren, pp. 103-107).

Private hunting trips were also offered to the wealthy and those obsessed to finished off what buffalo remained.

What food could Black Shawl cook? Buffalo were their livelihood.

Would civilization save Lakota culture?

The Lakota had no clocks to tell time. The sun did it for them. No astrological structures were designed by them to mark sun solstice or equinox.

No seeds were planted. No food was regularly produced to harvest annually. Crazy Horse and his wife, Black Shawl, and their group were the last American true hunter/gatherers.

Is it any wonder his wives needed cooking instructions when given flour, yeast, sugar and lard?

The Lakota diet was primarily wild meat for protein and corn they either traded or stole. Their stomachs were not accustomed to wheat flour, bread and high fat foods.

Lakota didn't raise hogs nor process lard.

When given flour and lard and taught to make Indian fry bread, it was tasty but was imbalanced nutrition--too high in starch and saturated fats.

The Lakota did not ferment fruits or grains, although Chinese fermented drinks 9,000 years ago.

Americans, like their European forefathers were conditioned to drinking alcoholic beverages. When given whiskey, Lakota easily got drunk, wanted more and would make inequitable and sometimes immoral trades for whiskey.

Is it any wonder Lakota confined to reservations without access to wild game developed health problems and many became alcoholics?

Were U.S. citizens any better than the Lakota?

Were the Lakota living a better life trying to establish their boundaries?

Were those controlling American coasts and closing in on the continent's middle more fitting for the Plains environment?

Who was better is a matter of perspective.

Lakota did not have schools. Schools were for those who had books and could read. Lakotans had neither. Do schools equal intelligence? No.

Lakota had to have superior memory and intelligence to survive in the semi-arid Plains. They moved based on food supply and the seasons.

As "uncivilized" generations passed, food preservation methods were all but forgotten as were making clothes and shelter from surrounding nature.

With the approaching twentieth-century, those living in permanent homes supplied from local stores with communications by mail or telegraph were ignorant of Lakota ways.

Policies developed and fighting ensued when neither understood each other's culture.

Maps were freely supplied by railroads enticing homesteaders. Meanwhile, Crazy Horse traveled through the Dakotas, Montana, Wyoming, Colorado, and Nebraska without a map.

Two cultures met at Fort Robinson Nebraska.

This background is provided to explain Crazy Horse's strategic autonomy. Marrying Nellie was needed to bridge his followers social shift from roaming to settled.

Crazy Horse figured that out.

Nellie had the Indian experiences taught by a Cheyenne mother. Her father provided skills to survive in settlements.

He needed to learn Nellie's experiences quickly if he was going to save his culture and have his own reservation with buffalo.

Crazy Horse knew Nellie had younger brothers and a couple older sisters. Two years after his death, one of her sisters would marry "The Man That Saved the Buffalo."

Chapter 23

Widows

Readers are encouraged to read the many books on the death of Crazy Horse.

How could there be so many versions?

Nobody has proven definitively who actually killed Crazy Horse.

How is that possible?

His tragic death happened on a military base. Soldiers were present. It happened in front of a military building. It happened surrounded by fifty, maybe a hundred Indian escorts and onlookers.

There are some things in common between the various versions.

For certain, Crazy Horse was stabbed with a knife, although it could have been two knives, or both stabbings were from a bayonet at the end of a soldier's rifle.

At the time of his death, Crazy Horse was carrying a knife. A version of the story claims he carried two knives. Were either the killing instruments?

There are many versions of Crazy Horse delivery to Fort Robinson and his stabbing. All generally conclude:

- He was surrounded by Lakotan—mostly opposed to him.
- He was not killed by long-time opponent, No Water.
- He was not brought into Fort Robinson in the sole custody of U.S. Army soldiers.
- He was accompanied by a mix group including Lieutenant Jesse M. Lee, his cousin Touch The Clouds, and some Indian scouts.
- His stabbing happened outside an Army barracks also used as a prison.
- He entered or was about to enter the barracks carrying at least one knife—perhaps two knives and possibly a pistol.

Was Crazy Horse being arrested by the Army?

If the arrest was true, it seems strange to me Crazy Horse was allowed to arrive with at least one weapon, a knife, and perhaps multiple weapons.

I spent seven and a half years in military intelligence and I never heard of a known prisoner being allowed to carry a weapon into his supposed jail.

After the arresting authority determines the person's identity, there are three basic steps to arrest:

1. Have probable grounds for arrest.
2. Inform the person they are being arrested.
3. Seize or touch the person's body when making the arrest.

From my readings, none of those things happened.

Although No Water and his followers retained bitterness toward Crazy Horse, that was not the cause of being delivered to the Army barracks.

Red Cloud and Spotted Tail were certainly frustrated with Crazy Horse and his notoriety though they apparently never publicly demanded his arrest.

The morning he was killed, Crazy Horse apparently made the decision to take Black Shawl from Red Cloud Agency to Spotted Tail Agency. What haunts me is the sentence from the book, **Crazy Horse--A Lakota Life**,

> "Until now Crazy Horse had been opposed to fleeing to Spotted Tail Agency where the Brule chief effectively controlled the northern Lakotas," (Bray, p. 363).

Research insinuates Crazy Horse was stabbed by an Army soldier when he fell back into the soldier's bayonet at the end of soldier's rifle, or that the soldier deliberately stabbed Crazy Horse in the back, perhaps twice.

Interestingly, the soldier's name was never confirmed by the Army and his name has only been speculation by Indians present.

At the time of the stabbing, there seems to be two active alternatives:

1. Was Crazy Horse being arrested? or
2. Was Crazy Horse being taken into protective custody?

Those are questions not resolved in the past 149 years, nor are those questions the point of this book.

Where were his wives?

Why wasn't Crazy Horse's wives brought to care for him after being stabbed?

Black Shawl, an unmarried girl in her twenties, was the first choice to care for Crazy Horse when he was shot in the face by No Water.

It seems a bit strange that after six years of marriage, and an expert in wound recovery, she was not immediately delivered from Spotted Tail Agency as soon as word was received of his stabbing.

Secondly, Nellie was at nearby Red Cloud Agency. Nellie was not sought to attend to her husband.

Why?

She was apparently abducted by Little Bear who thought he was to be Nellie's husband before she moved in with Crazy Horse a month or two before.

The timing of her abduction is bizarre.

Apparently it happened shortly before Crazy Horse was killed. Nellie had been in the family tipi with Worm, and Black Shawl.

Little Bear arrived with support (Red Shirt, High Bear, Apples, Eagle Horn) and called for Nellie. Worm came out and he was brushed aside, Crazy Horse's horse was shot.

> "(Little Bear…demanded that Nellie return with them. What the open abduction demonstrated in political terms was the determination…to force a crisis…(from a group) prepared to shoot him down," (Bray, p. 357).

Tragically, Crazy Horse was alone, just like when his mother took her life. His wives were not there to support him.

Sadly, important women remaining in Crazy Horse's life, his two wives, were not brought to him in the afternoon and evening hours between stabbing and death.

Can you imagine the frustration of Crazy Horse and his wives when they were restricted from seeing each other before death?

That was a three-way tragedy.

Immediately after Crazy Horse was stabbed, Fort Robinson surgeon, Dr. Valintine McGillicuddy, was brought to the scene. He attended to the injuries, but left Worm, Crazy Horse's father, to tend to the ceremonial details before and after death.

Like the last years and months of Crazy Horse life, his final hours, his death, his body preparation, and his burial, wives, Black Shawl and Nellie, were peripheral milieu.[33]

---

[33] Milieu is an English version of the 1800's French 'mi' (middle) '*lieu*" meaning place. That term would have been used by Nellie's French father. Wives had a place, respected in their community, but not in public.

Epilogue

Black Shawl-Crazy Horse and Nellie Larrabee-Crazy Horse lived fifty years beyond their husband's tragic death. His respect and world exposure grew as his wives faded from society.

A day before his killing, it was very likely, Crazy Horse anticipated his death which occurred on Fort Robinson. To insulate his wives, he ensured they lived in two separate camps about forty miles apart and not on Fort Robinson.

From the time of his surrender, very likely before, Crazy Horse dreamed of buffalo grazing on flowing-watered plains on his own reservation southeast of what is now Yellowstone National Park in Wyoming.

As his short life ended, trains, planes and automobiles began replacing horses.

Hope of a free-roaming Lakota died with the Ghost Dance. Yet, the dream of buffalo roaming the prairies was realized in a few decades. Through his wife's family connections and passion to restore the buffalo Crazy Horse's dream materialized.

It is estimated up to a half-million buffalo (American bison) graze today throughout the United States and Canada. Tens-of-thousands graze in the wild.[77]

Crazy Horse died but his buffalo restoration dream eventually came about through his wives.

Black Shawl (1845-1927)

Like a hero's footnote, Black Shawl, the loyal wife, has been ignored all these years. All heroes have support. Some gave little. Black Shawl gave her all.

Did she seek recognition? No.

Did she want it? Doubtful.

As a wife of a stature-bearing, bigger than life man, she needs to be given recognition and respect. I hope I have provided her a little of it in this review of her life.

Victor Swallow, a Pine Ridge Reservation native, told a story, *A Tribute to a Lakota Woman with Strong Lakota Values*, about Loretta Fern Laplante who was born in the early 1900s on the Cheyenne Indian Reservation.

Victor told of how Fern invited anyone to her door for coffee and food, how she cooked for local children, took in a daughter of a brother that had passed, how she was respected by whites and natives alike, and how she expressed compassion for the elderly.

Mr. Swallow, who grew up in a tent and cabin on the Reservation, wrote,

> "There are others among us that have qualities like Fern and as humble as they are never know how much they truly impact the world with their kind acts," (Swallow, p. 42).

I think Black Shawl was one of those kind, good-hearted Lakota woman.

It is assumed Black Shawl continued to live at the Spotted Tail Agency upon being widowed. Only eight short weeks after the death of Crazy Horse, Spotted Tail, the Brule leader, moved his Agency October 29, 1877, from northwest Nebraska to South Dakota which became the Rosebud Agency in 1878.

At some point Black Shawl may have moved to the Pine Ridge Reservation.

Though she suffered tuberculosis symptoms for many years, Black Shawl was able to live a relatively long life--to the age of eighty-two.

Black Shawl's brother, Red Feather, became a very supportive brother-in-law in skirmishes between 1871 and surrender in 1877 and was with Crazy Horse in the 1876 Battle of Little Bighorn.

The main medical doctor credited for treating Black Shawl's tuberculosis in 1877, and Crazy Horse on his deathbed the same year, was Dr. Valentine Trant McGillycuddy (1849-1939).

Dr. McGillycuddy served as surgeon for the U.S. Army when he was appointed Indian Agent in charge of the Pine Ridge Agency in South Dakota in 1879. As the first Surgeon General for South Dakota, he was adopted into the South Dakota Hall of Fame. The historic 1887 Valentine McGillycuddy House is now owned by Historic Rapid City. Upon death, McGillycuddy was cremated and his ashes were placed on Black Elk Peak. He was the first non-Indian to be placed there.[78]

Until her passing during an influenza epidemic in 1927, Black Shawl remained a widow and likely totally reliant on government "Indian" rations and health care.

Nellie Larrabee (1853-1928)

(Also known as Helen, Helena, Ellen, and Brown Eyes Woman with maiden name of Larrabee, Laravie, Larvie, married name: Nellie Larrabee-Crazy Horse.)

Nellie was the third child of Joseph Larrabee's first wife. He eventually had twelve children, seven were from Nellie's father's second wife (Mary Metcalf).

Nellie's siblings included: Julia Larvie Dunn (1850-1909), Sarah Laribee Philip (1851-1937), Elizabeth Ann

Larrabee Lafferty (1854-1910), Alexander Larvie (1858-1917), Philip Larvie (1858-1943), Zoe Larvie Utterback (1858-1950), William Larvie (1860-1950), Thomas Larvie Sr. (1863-1943), Rose Larvie Gerry (1870-1942), Joseph Larvie (1871-1921), and Richard "Kee-Ga-Lar" Larvie (1876-1950).

Joseph Larrabee was born September 3, 1825, in St. Charles, Missouri; baptized on September 8, 1826, at St. Charles Borromeo Catholic Church in St. Charles, Missouri, and is buried in St. Charles Catholic Cemetery, St. Francis, Todd County, South Dakota.

Nellie's father, Joseph, likely became independent because he lost his father, Joseph L'Arrivee, in July 1833 when he was seven years old. As a young man he traveled the Missouri River steamboats north to Dakota Territory. Eventually, he became a trader for the American Fur Trading Company when he married his first wife, a Cheyenne, Indian.

Since Joseph was French, he may have initially worked for the Hudson Bay Company which was the first corporation in North America.

Nellie was born on the Platte River Region of Wyoming in 1853. Joseph, her father, likely had a trading store near Fort Laramie, Wyoming. By 1849 Fort Laramie was a well-established Army station with affiliated traders and hang-around-the-fort Indians.

Nellie' mother, a Cheyenne Indian (name uncertain), was born in North Dakota. That is likely where Joseph met and married her while buying furs.

As a young girl, Nellie's father moved their young family of four girls, all under six years old, from Dakota Territory to what is now Montana. There, Joseph likely traded furs and pelts with the Crow Indians before moving to the Platte River valley near Fort Laramie Wyoming.

Nellie's brother, Alexander, was born in Montana sometime in November 1856.

Though speculating, it is likely Nellie's father, while living in Wyoming, married his second wife, Mary Elizabeth Metcalf-Larvie (1840-1898). She was also of Cheyenne ancestry, just like Nellie's birthmother.

Likely following the buffalo hide trade, by March 21, 1858, Joseph had moved his family to Nebraska where Lakota were concentrated around Army Forts. That is where Nellie's brother, Philip, was born to Joseph and Mary Elizabeth Medcalf-Larrabee.[34]

Northwest Nebraska was Nellie's home from age five until the Red Cloud Agency was moved to White River, South Dakota in October 1877. That was the

---

[34] Mary Elizabeth Medcalf was born in 1840 near Fort Laramie, Wyoming. Apparently, after losing his first wife between 1856-1857, Joseph quickly remarried Mary Elizabeth in need of a second wife to take care of his very young family.

month following her husband, Crazy Horse's death September 5, 1877.

The following year, 1878, the Red Cloud Agency moved to what became the Pine Ridge Indian Reservation.

It is likely Joseph Larrabee moved his Indian trading store (trading post) as a contingent of the large-scale Red Cloud Agency move.

Nellie remarried on an unknown date to Greasing Hand. Upon marriage to Nellie, he took the name, Albert Crazy Horse (1851-1933). Her second husband outlived her by five years and is also buried in the Catholic Mission Cemetery, (grave 2, section 15) in Wanblee, South Dakota.

Nellie died July 8, 1928 and is also buried in the Catholic Mission Cemetery in Wanblee, a small village on the Pine Ridge Indian Reservation.[79]

Nellie had no children from Crazy Horse. From her second husband Albert, who took the surname Crazy Horse, Nellie had a child, Julia Crazy Horse (August 1, 1901-January 18, 1978).

Nellie sent her daughter to boarding school in Rapid City. Thereafter, Julia married Hebert Holy Elk. After the passing of her mother, Julia got married to Paul Red Feather in 1929. On January 26, 1941, she married Jeff White.[80]

Julie, as a foster grandparent, lived in the Wolf Creek area east of Pine Ridge, South Dakota for most of her life. Julia is buried in Saint Ann's Cemetery, Wolf Creek, South Dakota.

Nellie had seven grandchildren: Ray Holy Elk (1919-1996), Alice Holy Elk Jack (1921-1989), Nancy Parie Holy Elk Crow (1923-1984), Elizabeth Velma Red Feather (1930-1993), Delores M. Red Feather Mills (19937-2005), Gertrude Holy Elk (-??-1920), and son Wallace.

Nellie, being half Cheyenne, likely drew Indian rations upon establishment of the Red Cloud camp after the Fort Laramie Treaty was signed in 1868.

After Nellie married Crazy Horse, and because Black Shawl was sickly, Nellie likely collected monthly rations for Crazy Horse, Black Shawl and herself when they were issued.

Black Shawl, weakened and sickly, likely allowed Nellie to do the family cooking.

Although it has been speculated that Nellie stole Crazy Horse's ration card after his death, it is likely Crazy Horse never actually collected rations for himself—that was women's work.

Nellie passed away in Pine Ridge, South Dakota July 8, 1928 and is buried in the Catholic Mission Cemetery, Wanblee, South Dakota.

(Photo by Gary Wietgrefe, cemetery, Wanblee, November 3, 2025.)

Of all the sisters and brothers-in-laws, Nellie brought to the Crazy Horse marriage, sister Sarah's marriage in 1879 to an American immigrant, James "Scotty" Philip, would have been the most interesting to Crazy Horse.

Scotty and Nellie's sister, Sarah, are the ones that helped to fulfill Crazy Horse's dream to restore the buffalo.

An important societal differentiation occurred to allow Sarah and Scotty Philip to restore buffalo.

The Civil War was over. Beef was in demand as cities grew, caravans headed west to California where meat was needed, and the Army needed meat for themselves and the Plains Indians.

Ten years before his death, Crazy Horse used force to keep cattle from moving north into the Dakotas.

> "Most of the first (Texas) cattle up the Chisholm Trail was destined for the Union Stockyards in Chicago. But some of them went …(north into the Plains), but there was little

> movement of cattle beyond the North Platte prior to 1868 because the Sioux under Red Cloud and Crazy Horse were blocking westward traffic toward Wyoming and Montana. These future states had been part of Dakota Territory…" (Lee & Williams, p. 21).

Ironically, Crazy Horse's father-in-law, Joseph Larrabee (1825-1890) and at least three of his brothers-in-laws became large South Dakota cattle ranchers. They included:

1. Michael Dunn (1845-1921) who married Joseph's daughter Julia;
2. James "Cornie" Utterback (1853-1939) who married Zoe; and
3. James "Scotty" Philip (1858-1911) who married Sarah (Robinson, 76).

Because Scotty Philip's cattle ranch was so successful, he was able to purchase South Dakota's last surviving herd of buffalo from Fred Dupree (1819-1898).

Dupree had rescued five bison calves on a hunt along the Grand River in 1881. July of that year was when Sitting Bull returned from his Canadian exile to settle on the Grand River of South Dakota.

Knowing that buffalo were about extinct, Fred Dupree kept all his buffalo calves and multiplied his herd to seventy-four.

Unknown to Dupree, Charles Goodnight, at the urging of his wife, Mary Ann Dyer-Goodnight (1839-1926) roped some buffalo calves in 1879 and grew their herd to forty-five by 1884 on a Lubbock, Texas ranch.

Goodnight's herd was known as the Southern Plains buffalo and Dupree's herd were Northern Plains which provided different genetics amongst a very small initial base.

I think Crazy Horse would have been very proud that his wife' sister, Sarah (who was half Cheyenne) and husband Scotty Philip who saved the last remaining buffalo in his hunting range.

Even more fortunate, Fred Dupree's wife, Mary, was part Lakota and French.

Scotty Philip and Fred Dupree were both large cattle ranchers. Dupree ranched north of the Cheyenne River in central South Dakota and Scotty Philip ranched south of the Cheyenne. They knew each other and likely had dinner together at each other's ranch. Their Indian wives would have cooked.

It is my contention that Mary Good Elk Woman-Dupree and Sarah Larrabee-Philip, and Mary Ann Dyer-Goodnight should receive much of the credit for saving the buffalo. For the year after Fred Dupree died, Scotty and Sarah Philip purchased the entire herd of seventy-four head from the Fred Dupree estate.

As an epilogue to **Women in the Life of Crazy Horse**, saving his cherished buffalo would have made Crazy Horse proud.

Had it not been for the homesteaders bringing cattle and sheep into the Plains to settle, there would not have been fences to restrain the buffalo. Buffalo fences had to be taller and stouter, but domestication saved buffalo from extinction.

There is one other major epilogue change that occurred to allow the Crazy Horse's name to live on through his wives, Black Shawl and Nellie Larrabee.

Not until Lakota were established on Reservations did they get a first name. It was assumed their name was both first and last (sur)name. Black Shawl therefore had no first name. When enrolled in Fort Robinson, her surname became Crazy Horse.

Following Christian and European tradition, first names were sought, and if not sought, they were assigned.

Writer of oral Lakota, Victor Swallow, in his story, *The Unexpected Destruction of Their Way of Life*, described name assignment this way,

> "The Government started enrolling natives. They were given first names. They asked one old fellow what name he wanted, and he said, "Jesus." They said he couldn't have that name, and asked what other name and he said, 'Mary,'" (Swallow, p. 107).

At the same time, women were assigned their husband's surname. Consequently, Black Shawl became Black Shawl-Crazy Horse and Nellie became Nellie Larrabee-Crazy Horse. Occasionally, it is easier to track wives and nineteenth century Lakota women through their husband's name (e.g. Crazy Horse).

Often wives' first names were not even included on Army's Indian enrollment. That followed tradition of U.S. Census where the family was tracked through the husband's name.

Postal communication was also through the husband's name.

If my great grandmother, Augusta Wietgrefe, (born in 1868) would have known Black Shawl in the summer of 1877, the young Augusta would have addressed a letter Mr. and Mrs. Crazy Horse, Fort Robinson, Nebraska. (There was no zip code back then.)

Even after Crazy Horse was killed the tradition of mail correspondence did not change. Consequently, if my great grandmother had planned a visit to Black Shawl in 1920, she would have addressed a penny postcard: Mrs. Crazy Horse, Mission, South Dakota. On the back side she may have written:

> "Dear Mrs. Crazy Horse, I hope you are feeling better. I will be arriving July 10 for a short visit. You have been in my thoughts and prayers. Yours truly. Mrs. Henry Wietgrefe"

I will use an actual example of how that tradition carried into the twenty-first century.

My father passed away in 1980. In the early 2000s, my mother would get Christmas and birthday cards from her cousins and friends addressed "Mrs. Walter Wietgrefe."[35]

Married women were known through their husbands. Fortunately for this book, I was able to track Rattling Blanket Woman, Black Buffalo Women, Black Shawl, and Nellie through Crazy Horse

Allowing only one wife was another cultural change that happened after the Rosebud and Pine Ridge Reservations were established.

Though the Morrill Anit-Bigamy Act of 1862 outlawed multiple marriages, Indians were not considered citizens until the Indian Citizenship Act of 1924. Technically, they could have multiple wives until then, but the nation's standards began to be applied to Lakota after the death of Crazy Horse.

Even though the U.S. Army was to enforce U.S. bigamy laws, that didn't mean Sioux tradition was ignored.

---

[35] Walter F. Wietgrefe, born in 1891 was my grandfather. In 1929 when my father Walter F. Wietgrefe was born, my grandfather added the suffix Sr. and my father Jr. Crazy Horse's father when he bestowed the name on his son in the mid-1850s simply changed his name to Worm.

Lieutenant Clark, the Army officer in charge of Crazy Horse, encourage the second marriage to Nellie, even though lawful wife, Black Shawl, was receiving Army allocated rations and medical care by none other than the Fort's head surgeon, Dr. McGillicuddy.

Background of Lakota marital relationships seem inconsequential. Much cultural dynamics has been lost.

Why?

Few cared to write down Lakota oral stories. Radio, television, books, magazines, the Internet and now social media are accepted forms of documented history.

I will again bring recognition to an octogenarian Lakota, Victor Swallow, who has passed on oral stories from his mother, who heard them from her mother, who got them from her mother's mother when Lakota roamed and lived in the wild.

In his story, *Looking Back into the Wild*, Mr. Swallow wrote about his great grandfather who had married sisters which parallel's Crazy Horse's father, Worm.

> "The government made my great Grandfather, One Crow, choose one of his two wives as his only wife. He chose Rebecca. Fannie married Joe White Plume and had more children" (Swallow, p. 157).

As Indian Agencies were formed followed by Reservations in the late 1800s into the 1900s (20th century), small towns were formed. Each had community centers. If the village was too small, people met in someone's home—just like when No Water arrived. Crazy Horse, Black Buffalo Woman, Touch The Cloud, and Standing Elk were meeting in the tipi of Black Bear and his wife.

Motorized vehicles replaced horses. More distant travel followed. Evening chats around campfires were extinguished. Community centers faded.

Now, technology allows social media, but it does not replace evening story time, dances into the late hours, jointly smoking pipes, discussions of tribal direction, and celebrations around campfires.

A century and a half since Crazy Horse was killed, technology has been adopted, food has become far more diverse and accessible, communication more universal, and transportation much quicker.

Fortunately, community events and memorial services, usually organized and food supplied by women, continue to reunite as a culture. Crazy Horse would smile.

As his oldest nephew, Red Fox, wrote,

> "In previous years I had seldom seen my great uncle, but after he went to the reservation, he occasionally visited our tipi and I remember listening to talks between him and my father. He

> was always kind.... My uncle, Chief Crazy Horse, who scorned life on the reservation, had won a place of leadership among all the Sioux," (Red Fox, pp. 45, 49).

I contend that Crazy Horse scorned reservation life because he knew the only way to restore his people and culture was to restore the buffalo—the most sustainable part of their lives.

This story has been a part of my life. As mentioned earlier my thirteen-year-old grandfather, his brother and father drove cattle in 1905 over 500 miles to our first farm in South Dakota. Six years later Scotty Philips died and his wife Sarah Larrabee-Philip eventually dispersed their buffalo herd.

What happened to the buffalo?

I will add some details of women I knew that carried on the legacy of building South Dakota huge buffalo herds. In the 1950s two such women were in my one-room school.

There were only nine or ten of us students in eight grades in that small school, but two girls (Lila Manfull and Irma Nagel) played important roles building and managing the remnants of Dupree's and Philip's buffalo.

My father (Walter Wietgrefe, Jr.) was working as a ranch-hand for Harry Manful in the late 1950s. Harry's daughter, Lila, married Jerry Houck (son of Roy Houck).

Remnants of Philip's herd was purchased by Roy Houck (also born in 1905). Roy was from Gettysburg, South Dakota. About ten miles northwest of their was where I started the first grade in a one-room school.

The winter of 1965-1966 was terrible with lots of snow—blizzard after blizzard.

Fortunately, when the Oahe Dam was being built on the Missouri River (completed in 1961) Roy Houck exchanged some of his Potter County ranch (east of the Missouri River) into Stanley County (west of the Missouri River). Several thousand acres of that grassland had been owned by Scotty and Sarah Philip.

Knowing Philips had good buffalo ground, Houck kept increasing his buffalo herd on what was known as "buffalo pasture." Thankfully he did.

After snow continued to pile up all winter of 1965 into '66, it was tough feeding cattle or buffalo. A March 1966 blizzard killed thousands of cattle—including many of Houck's.

Amazingly, Houck's buffalo survived. Why wouldn't they?

As Crazy Horse knew, buffalo had been grazing western South Dakota his whole life though blazing hot summers, droughts, and raging blizzards.

Houck named that area Triple U Buffalo Ranch. He expanded his buffalo herd and grassland into 60,000 acres and over 3,500 head of buffalo with the help of his son Jerry and wife Lila Houck.

Unfortunately, Jerry passed away in 1988. His father, Roy, was eighty-three which left Lila Manfull-Houck managing the massive buffalo operation.

The Triple U Buffalo Ranch, then the largest private buffalo herd in the world, was so well known that the 1988 novel, **Dances With Wolves** was turned into a 1990 western epic movie starring Kevin Costner.

Buffalo scenes in the movie were filmed at the Triple U Buffalo Ranch. Viewers can still watch the movie and relate to Crazy Horse amongst stampeding buffalo in the grasslands of western South Dakota.

As a schoolmate of Lila Manfull-Houck, I am so proud of her lifetime effort to manage their massive buffalo herd.

Lila was not my only one-room schoolmate to be closely involved with thousands of buffalo. Fellow honor goes to classmate Irma Nagel who married Thomas LeFaive who was manager of the 71,000 acre Custer State Park which for decades has the largest public herd of buffalo (1400-1500 head) in the world.

As Crazy Horse knew, buffalo in their native habitat are prolific.

To prevent over-grazing, rather than dangerously culling individual buffalo, starting in 1965 Custer State

Park had cowboys on horseback roundup the buffalo herds for sorting in reenforced corals.

Since the cowboys' job was very dangerous and they had to be excellent horsemen, no women were allowed on the annual Custer State Park Buffalo Roundup until 1979. That was when Irma Nagel-LeFaive became the first women to ever ride in the annual Buffalo Roundup.

I am happy to report my classmate Irma rode in three Buffalo Roundups.

This epilogue concludes realizing Crazy Horse's dream--survival of his people. In 1886 the total Dakota Territory (North and South Dakota) Indian population was 30,726 (Holley, p. 23). In the 2020 U.S. Census South Dakota alone had 98,842 Indians—more than a threefold increase in 134 years.[81]

Meanwhile, about 500,000 buffalo continue to roam in the U.S. Since Crazy Horse's death, no doubt women built upon his dream of having and nurturing children, promoting buffalo grazing and preparing buffalo dishes for Indians and whites alike.

It is my desire that readers of **Women in the Life of Crazy Horse** will have far more appreciation for the sincere, caring, hard-working, motherly, often lonely, brave, isolated, dejected and widowed women that kept family stories alive and made Lakota culture function.

They still do.

Bibliography and Notes

[1] Homer Ignatius "Wambli Haca" Chief Eagle, March 29, 1935-October 1, 1989, Find A Grave, https://www.findagrave.com/memorial/54173004/homer-chief_eagle.

[2] State v. Chief Eagle, Annotate this Case, 377 N.W.2d 141 (1985), STATE of South Dakota, Plaintiff and Appellee, v. Homer Ignatius CHIEF EAGLE, Defendant and Appellant, No. 14752, Supreme Court of South Dakota, considered on Briefs May 23, 1985, decided November 20, 1985, https://law.justia.com/cases/south-dakota/supreme-court/1985/14752-1.html.

[3] Bray, Kinglsey M., Notes on the Crazy Horse Genealogy, Part 2: Miscellaneous notes on the Crazy Horse Miniconjou Connection, 2006, parts One and Two.

[4] Matson, William B., Crazy Horse, The Lakota Warrior's Life & Legacy, by the Edward Clown Family, Gibbs Smith (press), Layton, UT, First Edition, 2016, pp. 16, 17, 21, 32-35, 68-70, 87, 131, 136-138, 202.

[5] Bray, Kingsley M., Crazy Horse—A Lakota Life, University of Oklahoma Press, Norman, OK, 2006, pp. 5-6, 10-12, 130, 143, 145-147, 157, 297, 318-322, 363.

[6] American Indian History, The Life of Crazy Horse, https://americanindiancoc.org/american-indian-history-the-life-of-crazy-horse/.

[7] Beads, South Dakota Timeline, https://www.ereferencedesk.com/resources/state-history-timeline/south-dakota.html

---

[8] Verendrye plaque, is now displayed at the Cultural Heritage Center, 900 Governors Drive, Pierre, South Dakota.

[9] King, James Otto, Waneta, The Charger: Dakota War Chief, English Captain in the War of 1812, The First Scout, Ochethi Shakowin, History and Culture, Dakota Win, March 23, 2011, https://thefirstscout.blogspot.com/2011/03/waneta-charger-dakota-war-chief-english.html.

[10] Fort Pierre Chouteau, City of Fort Pierre, South Dakota, https://www.fortpierre.com/fort-pierre-tourism-information/history/

[11] Kappler, Charles J., et al., US Government Documents Related to Indigenous Nations, Treaty of Fort Laramie, National Endowment for the Humanities, https://commons.und.edu/indigenous-gov-docs/158/

[12] Mustful, Colin, Ceding Contempt—Minnesota's Most Significant Historical Event, Lulu Publishing Services, 2016, pp. 27-28.

[13] Riggs, Stephan Return, 1812-1883 Missionary to the Dakota Indians, Boston University, School of Theology, History of Missiology, https://www.bu.edu/missiology/missionary-biography/r-s/riggs-stephen-return-1812-1883/.

[14] Myers, Philip Van Ness, Ancient History, revised edition, Ginn & Company, 1904, pp. 4, 5.

[15] Holley, Frances Chamberlain, Once Their Home, Our Legacy from the Dahkotahs, published by Donohue & Henneberry, Chicago, Copyright, 1890, pp. 23, 27-28, 32.

[16] Cameron, Anne, Daughters of Copper Women, Harbour Publishing, 2002, p. 112.

---

[17] Driving Hawk-Sneve, Virginia, Sioux Woman—Traditionally Sacred, South Dakota Historical Society Press, Pierre, SD, 2016, pp. 3, 21, 23.

[18] Sioux Creation Myth, The Sioux Tribe, https://siouxtribefactsandlegends.weebly.com/creation.html.

[19] Welmore, Helen Cody, Buffalo Bill—The Last of the Great Scouts, the life story of Colonel William F. Cody, First Bison Books, copyright 1965 reproduced from the 1899 edition, p. 184.

[20] Akta Lakota, Lakota Emergence Story, Akta Lakota Museum and Cultural Center, St. Joseph's Indian School, Chamberlain, South Dakota, https://aktalakota.stjo.org/lakota-legends/lakota-emergence-story/.

[21] Wietgrefe, Gary W., Relating to Ancient Learning—as it influences the 21st century, GWW Books, 2018, p. 294.

[22] Eggleston, Edward, A First Book in American History—with special reference to Lives and Deeds of Great Americans, by D. Appleton and Company, 1889, p. preface.

[23] Johnson, Willis E., South Dakota—A Republic of Friends, The Capital Supply Company, Pierre, SD, 1915, p. 8.

[24] Swallow, Victor, Lakota Life After the Buffalo—Life and Times of Victor Swallow, transcribed by Vikki Swallow, published by GWW Books, Rapid City, SD, 2025, pp. 13, 6, 8-9, 42, 46, 63-64, 107,110-111, 157.

[25] Fisher, Richard, D., Copper Canyon Mexico, and the Children of Kokopelli, in article Mysterious Water Features and Utensils from Across Pre-Columbian North America—Long Distance Heavy Weight, magazine article Creel, Copper Canyon, Mexico, copyright 2004, no page numbers.

[26] Longstreet, Stephen, Indian Wars of the Great Plains, copyright 1970 republished under the title, War Cries on Horseback, Indian Head Books, 1993, p. 5.

[27] Myers, John Myers, The Saga of Hugh Glass—Pirate, Pawnee, and Mountain Man, University of Nebraska Press, First Bison Book Printing, copyright 1963 reprinted 1976, p. 147.

[28] McDougall, Christopher, Born to Run—A Hidden Tribe, Super Athletes, and the Greatest Race the World Has Ever Seen, by Alfred A. Knoff publisher, 2010, p. 15.

[29] Billy Mills, Wikipedia, https://en.wikipedia.org/wiki/Billy_Mills.

[30]Lemly, H.R., U.S. Army Lieutenant, "The Death of Crazy Horse," New York Sun, September 14, 1877.

[31] Hinman, Eleanor H., Oglala Sources on the Life of Crazy Horse, University of Nebraska stenographer, interview with He Dog (Sunka Bloka), Thomas White Cow Killer, interpreter, July 7, 1930, Oglala, South Dakota, p. 10, 14.

[32]Hedren, Paul L., After Custer, Loss and Transformation in Sioux Country, University of Oklahoma Press, Norman, OK, 2011, pp. 96, 99, 103-107,144, 164.

[33] Miller, Mark, The Singing Wire—a Story of the Telegraph, John C. Winston Company, First Edition, 1953, pp. x, 47-49.

[34]Sandoz, Mari, Crazy Horse: The Strange Man of the Oglala, (1942) republished by University of Nebraska Press with introduction by Stephen B. Oates, 1992, pp. 113-118.

[35]Sajna, Mike, Crazy Horse, The Life Behind the Legend, Castle Books, 2000, (taken from 2005 edition), pp. 156-159, 226-229, 309.

---

[36]Chief Crazy Horse, Lakota Sioux Nation President, Chief Liquidated in Cold Blood by the United States of America, https://www.americanussr.com/american-ussr-crazy-horse.html.

[37] Alchetron.com. See https://alchetron.com/Black-Buffalo-Woman.

[38]Keys, Jim, The History Harrold, Crazy Horse, April 15, 2013, https://thehistoryherald.com/articles/american-history/civil-war-american-indian-wars-pioneers-1801-1900/crazy-horse/2/.

[39]Wietgrefe, Gary W., Lessons of an Immigrant Father—1905 cattle drive 500 miles to Dakota, GWW Books, 2025, p. viii.

[40]Wetmore, Helen Cody, Buffalo Bill, the Last of the Great Scouts, The life and story of Colonel William F. Cody, Bison Book, April, 1965, edition, p. 157. Note, Helen Wetmore was a sister of William Cody.

[41]Hardorff, Richard D., The Death of Crazy Horse: A Tragic Episode in Lakota History, He Dog interview by Mari Sandoz June 30, 1931, p. 118.

[42]Red Cloud Agency: I caution readers about the term "Red Cloud Agency." It is a term I have previously used interchangeably with Red Cloud's camp and Red Cloud Agency. Actually, Red Cloud's Agency was not officially established until 1871. Red Cloud had a large camp after the Red Cloud War ended in 1868.

Once his Agency was official, Red Cloud administered the growing population of mainly Oglala Lakota, Northern Cheyenne, and Arapaho that straggled in under subchiefs between 1871 and 1878.

Red Cloud's camp likely moved several times between 1868 and 1871 in an area of what is now the far southwest South Dakota, far northwest Nebraska, and the southeastern border of Wyoming.

In 1871 the Red Cloud Agency moved from near Fort Laramie (in southeast Wyoming) to near For Robinson, Nebraska (in August 1873). The third official move of the Red Cloud Agency was to South Dakota on the White River in October 1877.

Finally, the Red Cloud Agency was officially dissolved and members dispersed to the Pine Ridge Reservation in 1878 which is still in existence.

[43]Biblical Commandments are part of Lakota culture. (See Exodus 5:13-14, and16-17, New King James Version.) The Fifth Commandment, "You shall not murder;" The Sixth Commandment, "You shall not commit adultery;" and "You shall not bear false witness against thy neighbor," were each violations of not only of Biblical Commandments, but also tribal custom.

There is one more Commandment that comes to mind—the Eighth. I have not detected false statements, but anger. In Biblical terms, the violation of the Eighth Commandment was speaking badly about another person. "But I say to you, love your enemies, bless those who curse you, do good to those who hate you, and pray for those who spitefully use you and persecute you, that you may be sons of your Father in heaven; (Matthew 5:44-45). Lakota honesty was a firm practice.

Tenth Commandment states, "You shall not covet your neighbor's wife," (Exodus 20:17, New King James Version). The controversy and tribal resolution of Crazy Horse taking No

---

Water's wife confirms tribal culture agrees with Biblical doctrine about taking someone else's spouse.

[44] War Bride was a term for a military member (mostly servicemen, but also women) to return to the U.S. from serving in a foreign country with their legal wife, or even fiancé. See https://immigrationhistory.org/item/war-brides-acts-1945-1947/.

[45] Albers, Patricia, and Beatrice Medicine, The Hidden Half: Studies of Plains Indian Women, University Press of American, 1983, explained writings of Ella Cara Deloria's book Speaking of Indians, pp. 238, 242.

[46] Brown, Bruce, He Dog Remembers Crazy Horse #2--An Oglala Sioux's recollections of his old friend, Astonisher.com Library, as interviewed by Eleanor Hinman and Mari Sandoz, John Colhoff, Interpreter, July 13, 1930, updated April 6, 2011, https://astonisher.com/archives/museum/he_dog_hump.html#black_twin.

[47] Lee, Wayne, C., Scotty Philip, The man who saved the Buffalo, The Caxton Printers, Ltd., Caldwell, Idaho, 1975, p. 54, 89, 115-116, 118.

Note that Helen, a.k.a. Nellie, was actually the third oldest Larrabee daughter.

[48]Find a Grave, Joseph Laravie, https://www.findagrave.com/memorial/98911685/joseph-larvie.

[49] Badlands, Early Indians and Explorers, History of the Badlands National Monument, National Park Service. French explorers preceded the Lakota in western South Dakota by more than a century. Quoting this reference,

"For more than a century prior to 1763, the upper Missouri Valley, including what is today Badlands National Monument, was under French Control. Under terms of the Treaty of Paris of 1763 French possessions west of the

---

Mississippi River were ceded to Spain. Spain returned the area, known as Louisiana, to France in 1800 in the secret Treaty of San Ildefonso. In 1803 the entire region, which included all of the present states of Arkansas, Missouri, Iowa, Nebraska, and South Dakota, plus parts of eight other states was purchased by the United States from France for $15,000,000."

[50] The Cultural Heritage Center, What tribes were in South Dakota? "No one really knows what tribes lived in South Dakota before about A.D. 1500, other than the ancestors of the Arikara and Mandan.

"While there is some debate among archaeologists, and historians, it is generally felt that, during the 1500s and 1600s, ancestors of the Apaches, Kiowas, Kiowa-Apaches, Arapahos and Comanches inhabited parts of western South Dakota during the course of their southward migrations.

"The Crow tribe also lived in western South Dakota. Central South Dakota at that time was the homeland of the Arikaras, Mandans, and, for at time, the Cheyenne.

"Eastern South Dakota was occupied by the Lakota, Omahas, Poncas, and perhaps Iowas and Otos.

"By the 1700s, the Chyenne moved west, followed by the Lakota.

"The Mandans moved wholly into North Dakota, and eventually so did the Akikara.

"The Poncas and Omahas moved south into Nebraska, displaced by bands of eastern Sioux, the Dakota and Nakota peoples, moving into South Dakota from Minnesota.

"By the mid-1800s, the Sioux peoples occupied virtually the entire state."

[51] The Black Hills Souvenir: A pictorial and historic description of the Black Hills, 1902.

[52] Lee, Bob, and Dick Williams, Last Grass Frontier—The South Dakota Stock Growers Heritage, sponsored by the South Dakota Stock Growers Association, Black Hills

---

Publishers, Inc., Sturgis, South Dakota, copyright 1964, pp. 21, 159.

[53] Robinson, James M., The Wild World of James (Scotty) Philip West From Fort Pierre, Western Lore Press Los Angeles, California, 1974, pp. 61, 76.

[54] Kloberdanz, Timothy J., Remembering Elbridge Gerry—Frontier hero had ties to a signer of the Declaration of Independence, Roundup Magazine, April 2026, pp. 12-13.

[55] Red Fox, The Memoirs of Chief Red Fox with an Introduction by Cash Asher, A Fawcett Crest Book, Fawcett Publications, Inc., 1972, pp. 43-45, 49.

[56]Frank Benjamin Grouard (a.k.a. Standing Bear), (1850-1905) was the son of a Mormon missionary. As a boy he was captured by the Crow, either traded or captured by Sioux where he spent the next decade. Eventually, he became an interpreter for the U.S. Army reporting to General George Crook, who became U.S. Army Head of Department of the Platte from 1875-1882 when Crazy Horse surrendered.

[57] History of Rapid City, Rapid City Public Library, https://rapidcitylibrary.org/history-of-rapid-city.

[58] Fire Thunder, Alex, Lakota Voices from the Archives—the Fire Thunder Narratives recorded by Ella C. Deloria, a 1930s Dakota anthropologist and linguist, South Dakota History, Volume 55, Number 4, winter 2025, p. 286.

[59] Buecker, Thomas, R., Fort Robinson and the American West, 1874-1899, included the story Final Days of Crazy Horse, copyright 1999, as summarized in "Friends of the Little Bighorn Battle." Buecker was curator of the Ft. Robinson Museum, https://friendslittlebighorn.com/crazyhorsedeath.htm.

[60] Brommel, Allen, Rev. Stephan R. Riggs, Missionary to the Dakota Indians, Biography of Missionaries, Volume 88, Issue 17, 2012, https://sb.rfpa.org/rev-stephen-r-riggs-missionary-to-the-dakota-indians/.

[61] The US-Dakota War of 1862, Reverend Stephen and Mary Riggs, https://www.mnhs.org/usdakotawar/stories/history/reverend-stephen-and-mary-riggs.

[62] Legacy Thomas L. Riggs, South Dakota Hall of Fame, Programs Directory Site, 1978, https://www.sdexcellence.org/Thomas_L._Riggs_1978.

[63] Neihardt, John G., Black Elk Speaks, The Complete Edition, University of Nebraska Press, 2014, pp. 53, 317.

[64] Anderson, Harry H., Crazy Horse Surrender Ledger Forward, Nebraska State Historical Society publication by Harry H. Anderson Milwaukee County Historical Society Milwaukee, Wisconsin, https://history.nebraska.gov/publications_section/crazy-horse-surrender-ledger-foreward/.

[65] Keller, Robert H. Jr, Episcopal Reformers and Affairs at Red Cloud Agency, 1870-1876," Nebraska History 68 (1987): 116-126, https://history.nebraska.gov/wp-content/uploads/2017/12/doc_publications_NH1987Reformers.pdf.

[66] Black Shawl, Wikipedia, The Free Encyclopedia, footnote reference Richard G. Hardorff, The Surrender and Death of Crazy Horse: A Source Book about a Tragic Episode in Lakota History, Author H. Clarke Company,1998 edition, p. 43.

[67] Sex Ratio at Birth, Our World in Data, https://ourworldindata.org/grapher/sex-ratio-at-birth.

---

[68] Indian hammers and horse hobbles: Although Plains Indians used rocks as hammers for pounding stakes and smaller ones as tomahawks, most were used as horse hobbles.

Without fences, horses could graze comfortably, but if they tried to run away, which was common when trying to be caught, the oblong rock hung around the neck by a leather strap would swing and hit the horse's knees allowing Indians, usually boys, to catch them.

[69] Markley, Bill, and Kellen Cutsforth, Old West Showdown—Two Authors Wrangle over the Truth About the Mythic Old West, Two Dot, Helena, MT, p. 103.

[70] Hilleary, Cecily, Florida Prison Fort Served as Testing Ground for Federal Indian Boarding School System, November 1, 2021, https://www.voanews.com/a/florida-prison-fort-served-as-testing-ground-for-federal-indian-boarding-school-system/6290866.html. The problem with the Florida scenario was that the well-known Geronimo and Naiche, Apache chiefs, were not imprisoned in Florida until 1886. However, through various chiefs with Army connections, Crazy Horse may have heard that Comanche and Southern Cheyenne leaders, rather than being executed after the Texas Red River War of 1875, were imprisoned in Florida until their sentences were completed in 1878.

[71] Veglahn, Nancy, The Buffalo King—the story of Scotty Philip, published by Charles Scribner's Sons, New York, 1971, p. 45.

[72] Crazy Horse, Immediate Family, Wikipedia, https://en.wikipedia.org/wiki/Crazy_Horse.

[73] Crazy Horse, Military History, Fandom, https://military-history.fandom.com/wiki/Crazy_Horse.

[74] Brennan, Kristine, Crazy Horse, Famous Figures of the American Frontier, Chelsea House Publishers, 2001. Also,

Garnett, William, Čháŋ Óhaŋ Lakota (abt. 1840 - 1877), https://www.wikitree.com/wiki/Lakota-29.

[75] Tiwahe, Tashunke Witko, Facebook post under Tashunke Witko Tiwahe/Crazy Horse Family/ECF, https://www.facebook.com/search/top/?q=A%20facebook%20post%20Mar.%2022%202024%3A%20Nellie%20Larrabee%20was%20presented%20to%20Crazy%20Horse%20by%20Lt%20William%20Clark%20.

[76] Lilly, Elizabeth, X post, May 11, 2024, https://x.com/ChitkwesuManetu/status/1789338322696847374.

[77] Bison Population by State, 2026, World Population Review, https://worldpopulationreview.com/state-rankings/bison-population-by-state.

[78] McGillycuddy, Valentine Trant, Doctor, February 14, 1849-June 6, 1939, Historic Rapid City, https://www.historicrc.org/pagemg .

[79] Ellen "Nellie" Larabee Crazy Horse, Find a Grave, Catholic Mission Cemetery, Grave 2, Section 15, Wamblee, South Dakota, https://www.findagrave.com/memorial/13090554/ellen-crazy_horse.

[80] Julia Crazy Horse White, Find A Grave, https://www.findagrave.com/memorial/152906823/julia-white.

[81]Klinski, Michael, Does South Dakota have the highest percentage of Native American residents?, Brief Fact, South Dakota Newswatch, December 18, 2025.

Index

C

D

E

F

G

M

N

S

T

Y

Other Books by Gary W. Wietgrefe

- Lessons of an Immigrant Father, 1905 cattle drive 500 miles to Dakota
- Humor and Learning in a One-Room School
- Relating to Ancient Culture, and the mysterious agent changing it
- Relating to Ancient Learning, as it influences the 21st century
- Destination North Pole, 5000 km by bicycle
- Lakota Life After the Buffalo (by Victor Swallow)
- Living Beyond Fate (by Wesley N. Wietgrefe)
- Dakota Country Poems
- Life in Flight (Dakota poems)
- Proso Millet: A Farmer's Guide
- Proso Millet: A Trade Summary

www.ingramcontent.com/pod-product-compliance
Lightning Source LLC
Jackson TN
JSHW080740140526
102249JS00004B/9

* 9 7 9 8 9 9 4 1 9 6 8 2 3 *